UMARU IBRAHIM FCIB, mni
The Accomplished Public Servant

UMARU IBRAHIM FCIB, mni
The Accomplished Public Servant

GAMBO DORI

Safari Books Ltd.
Ibadan

Published by
Safari Books Ltd.
Ile Ori Detu
1, Shell Close
Onireke
Ibadan.
Email: safarinigeria@gmail.com
Website: http://safaribooks.com.ng

© 2021, Gambo Dori
First Published 2021

All rights reserved. This book is copyright and so no part of it may be reproduced, stored in a retrieval system, or transmitted, in any form or by any means, electrical, mechanical, electrostatic, magnetic tape, photocopying, recording or otherwise, without the prior written permission of the author.

ISBN: 978-978-58008-6-9 Cased
       978-978-58008-7-6 Paperback

Contents

Foreword.. vii
Acknowledgements... ix

CHAPTER ONE: THE EARLY YEARS 1
- The Roots-Gaya and Wudil..................... 1
- Family Background................................ 1
- The Gyanawa Clan................................. 2
- Mallam Ahmad Leaves Kasauni.............. 3
- Alkali Ibrahim Ahmad............................ 4
- The Birthplace: Gaya 6
- Movement to Wudil 7
- The Beginning of Western Education for Umaru... 8
- Movement to Kano................................. 9
- Kano City of the 1960s........................... 10
- Back to School 12
- Secondary School 13
- Become a Graduate 17
- NYSC in Rivers State 22
- Port Harcourt... 24
- Life in Port Harcourt.............................. 26

CHAPTER TWO: THE KANO STATE CIVIL SERVICE... 29
- Beginnings in Kano Civil Service............. 29
- Probing the Ousted Government............. 31
- The Family - The Rock............................ 34

- The Abubakar Rimi Era............................... 37
- The Rimi Administration........................... 39
- Rimi's Radical Moves................................ 41
- Secondment to WRECA............................ 44
- Becoming a Permanent Secretary.............. 48
- A Change of Turf: From Kano Civil
  Service to the Banking Sector.................... 52

CHAPTER THREE: NIGERIA DEPOSIT INSURANCE CORPORATION (NDIC)....................... 59
- A New Beginning at NDIC......................... 59
- Getting Started.. 60
- Stormy Days in the Banking Sector........... 64
- Sojourn in the National Institute............... 69
- NDIC - The Millenium Years..................... 76
- Movement within the Corporation............ 82
- Preparation for Retirement........................ 85
- At the Helm of Affairs................................ 86
- NDIC under Umaru Ibrahim..................... 87

CHAPTER FOUR: IN THE EYES OF OTHERS............. 103

INDEX... 109

Foreword

It gives me great pleasure to introduce this book on the life and times of Umaru Ibrahim, the Managing Director of the Nigeria Deposit Insurance Corporation (NDIC).

I have known Umaru Ibrahim since we attended the same Primary School where I was a year ahead of him. He attended Rumfa College in Kano City, while I attended Government College, Keffi, in present day Nasarawa State. We still interacted closely, however, when I was home for the holidays. We later both attended Ahmadu Bello University, Zaria where we continued to bond.

Umaru Ibrahim has had a distinguished public service career, which we are proud to be associated with. He had the unique versatility of rising to the top of the two public services he served. In the first part of his career in the Kano State Government, Umaru played key roles, particularly in the Cabinet Office, and the Water Resources and Engineering Construction Agency (WRECA), a government parastatal. His high levels of competence and integrity were recognized. It was not surprising therefore, that, in the space of only ten years, Umaru rose to the highest position of Permanent Secretary.

After reaching the pinnacle of his career and paying his dues to his State he transferred his services to the banking sector as a foundation management staff of the NDIC. He worked hard to contribute to building the institution, as a crowning mark of which he, ultimately, became the Managing Director, serving for two consecutive terms.

Our paths officially crossed again in 1999, when I was appointed the Deputy Governor of the Central Bank of Nigeria. It was a period of global financial turbulence, during which we worked closely with the NDIC, through many salutary interventions, to stabilize the banking sector. When I was the Minister of Finance, 2007-2009, NDIC was an important agency of the ministry where I had the pleasure of working with outstanding public servants like Umaru Ibrahim and his colleagues. This close association continued even when I was Minister of National Planning 2009-2013.

Today, I am pleased to note the big strides NDIC has made under his leadership as Managing Director. There is no doubt that he has maintained the tempo started by his predecessors, the founding fathers of NDIC, both of whom I had the pleasure to work closely with. Of particular note is the innovative introduction of bridge-banking as a failure resolution mechanism by the NDIC under his watch, which has helped to protect depositors' funds, as well as jobs in the banking sector.

NDIC is now more visible, with its brand recognised both at home and abroad. Under Umaru Ibrahim's leadership, the NDIC has also met the stringent requirements for certification by the British Standards Institution (BSI). In recognition of the stellar performance of the NDIC at the local and international levels, Umaru was elected in 2013 as a member of the Executive Council of the International Association of Deposit Insurers (IADI), based in Basel, Switzerland. This is a forum for deposit insurers from around the world to share experience and benefit from one another in the field of deposit insurance.

I recommend to the reader this well-written book that both chronicles the life of this unique public servant, Umaru Ibrahim and his tenure as Chief Executive Officer of the NDIC, where he spent the greatest part of his career.

DR. SHAMSUDDEEN USMAN

Acknowledgements

I wish to acknowledge with thanks the contributions made by institutions and individuals to the writing of this biography. I single out the Nigeria Deposit Insurance Corporation (NDIC) for giving me both the opportunity and the resources to undertake the exercise of recording the life of one of its longest serving staff and Managing Director. Throughout the duration of writing this book NDIC adopted me as one of its own readily giving me access to narration and documents that assisted a great deal to the success of this project. I make particular mention of Dr. J. Ade Afolabi, Dr. Sunday Oluyemi, Mustafa Mohammed Ibrahim and Dr. Hashim Ibrahim Ahmad whom at various times were at the helm of affairs in the Research Department.

Writing a book of this nature is a collaborative effort. I am very grateful to those who assisted me to interview various personalities associated with Alhaji Umaru Ibrahim. These include Ismael Bala of English Department, Bayero University, Kano who helped to interview the relations and friends in Kano and Ibrahim Kabiru Sule, then a reporter with Daily Trust newspaper, now with National Open University of Nigeria (NOUN), with whom we spent many days interviewing Alhaji Umaru sometimes in the office and other times at home. There is Prince Dotun Oyelade whom I invited from his base in Ibadan and who made very useful contributions to the final draft.

I also thank Alhaji Umaru's relations, childhood friends, classmates, tutors and mentors who have granted me access to interact with them and learn about Alhaji Umaru's formative years. My thanks in this category goes to Mallam Yahaya Hamma, Dr. Shamsuddeen Usman, Dr. Abba Abdullahi, late Sarki Gwarzo, Professor Munzali Jibril, Dr. Joseph Garba Donli, Engr. Baba Gana Zanna, Professor Ali Danlami Yahaya, Dr. Haroun Al Rashid Adamu, Garba Yusuf Imam and Mallam Bashari Ibrahim.

I am also grateful to Dr. Nuradeen Auwal of Baze University Abuja and Professor Ismaila Tsiga of Bayero University Kano for their professional guidance at various stages of this project.

CHAPTER ONE

THE EARLY YEARS

The Roots-Gaya and Wudil

The journey for Umaru Ibrahim to the pinnacle of the Nigeria Deposit Insurance Corporation (NDIC) started in the dusty town of Gaya, some fifty kilometers north-east of Kano, where he was born in 1950. He was the first born to his mother, Saudatu and the second male child for his father. His father, Alkali Ibrahim Ahmed was then posted as a mufti in Gaya, one of the principal outposts in the Kano province.

Family Background

Alkali Ibrahim, Umaru Ibrahim's father, was a very well-regarded, learned and disciplined scholar. He had initially been educated in the traditional ways under the watchful eyes of his father, Mallam Ahmad, who ran a Qur'anic School in Gwangwazo quarters of Kano city where Ibrahim was born. Mallam Ahmad was also the resident teacher of Mai Babban Daki Mariya, the mother of the late Abdullahi Bayero, the Emir of Kano, who reigned between 1925 and 1953. Mallam Ahmad was initially based in Kausani village in Wudil Local Government Area where he was born and raised in the homestead of Mallam Ahmad Sa'alabi who was also running a Qur'anic School there.

Mallam Ahmad Sa'allabi took over the school from Mallam Dikkoye, his father. Mallam Dikkoye, who was a blind but learned Fulani teacher, migrated from Tsangaya village, now under Albasu village, to Kasauni. He settled in Kasauni and established an Islamic school where he taught the Qur'an, the Fiqh and Islamic studies together with his son Ahmad Sa'alabi. When Mallam Dikkoye died, Mallam Sa'alabi took over the school; he subsequently became the village Imam.

The Gyanawa Clan

Mallam Dikkoye, the patriarch of the family, was of the Gyanawa clan of Tsangaya village. The Gyanawa was one of the Fulani clans who had settled in the eastern part of Kano emirate, particularly in the hamlets around Gaya. They had acquired Islamic education and had become settled as teachers, Imams, and jurists in these towns and villages. During Jihad, which was started by Sheikh Usman Dan Fodio, a fellow Fulani kinsman, they were not only able to contribute fighting men but gave solid intellectual support to the revolution. At the end of the Jihad which saw the Fulani emerge victorious, the Fulani took over the reins of government in Kano and other parts of the caliphate. It was inevitable that the leadership of the critical areas of government like the judiciary and the religious centres would be populated by the Mallams from the Gyanawa clan. Due to their educational qualifications, members of the Gyanawa clan have been acknowledged to have played a significant role in the history of Kano as scholars and administrators of justice. Only two of the 19th Century Chief Qadis of Kano were not from the Gyanawa clan.

Mallam Ahmad Leaves Kasauni

Mallam Ahmad was a frequent visitor to Kano city from Kasauni. The reason for his frequent visits was to seek and acquire deeper knowledge and exposure in Islamic studies. On these journeys, he was always in the company of his son, Ibrahim, Umaru's father. As the visits became more and more frequent, he took the decision to permanently settle down in Kano. He found a suitable place in Dan Agundi quarters that was adequate to accommodate his growing family as well as to start another Qur'anic School. He settled there with his family and the students that followed him. As time went by, the population of the school increased greatly, attracting more students of all ages from every nook and cranny of Kano. Mallam Ahmad was very learned in Qur'anic studies and the fiqh, a rare feat then.

Mallam Ahmad's Qur'anic School flourished and as his reputation grew, he attracted the attention of Maibabban Daki Mariya, the mother of the Emir of Kano, late Abdullahi Bayero (1926-1953), who lived in Gwangwazo quarters very close to Dan Agundi. She wanted a learned Mallam to teach all aspects of the Qur'an and the fiqh to her and her large household. Mallam Ahmad was invited to her house and later appointed as a teacher. He then had to move both his household and the school from Dan Agundi to a house Maibabban Daki had provided in Gwangwazo quarters. He became her personal teacher and adviser and due to this closeness to the emir's mother, he was also well accepted in the palace. When Mallam

Ahmad died, his son Mallam Ibrahim, succeeded him and moved into his late father's residence.

Alkali Ibrahim Ahmad

Alkali Ibrahim Ahmad followed in the footsteps of his illustrious progenitors. He was intelligent, hardworking, and had the opportunity to have acquired his education at the feet of his father, Mallam Ahmad. As it was also the practice then in the traditional system he also gained from attending tutorials based on the teachings of erudite Mallams that abound in Kano. When the colonial government wanted to start a judicial school named School of Arabic School, in Kano, he saw himself as a promising young man who could benefit from such training, considering his good grounding in Islamic knowledge and jurisprudence.

In actual fact, the idea of establishing the Kano law school was a brilliant conception of the late Emir Abdullahi Bayero, who, on his way to Mecca for pilgrimage by road, visited that kind of school in Sudan. The emir could be conveniently said to belong to the class of notable and visionary rulers who were ahead of their time. This, coupled with the fact that he presided over one of the most buoyant treasuries in Nigeria during that period, made it possible for him to prosecute and achieve the rapid development of Kano city. It is on record that it was during his reign that Kano city joined the prestigious league of cities which have electricity and pipe-borne water supply to the homes of its inhabitants.

The emir was highly impressed with what he saw in the law school he visited in Sudan which gave instructions in advanced training in Sharia law and he thought it would be beneficial if such a school was built in Kano as it would take care of the shortage of trained personnel in the Sharia legal system in his emirate. Therefore, when he returned from Mecca, he made recommendations to the colonial government for the establishment of such a school in his domain. The colonial government gave him the go-ahead to establish the school after a close and diligent study of his proposal. The school was subsequently established and before long, it attracted students from Kano and all over the Northern region of the country.

By the time Mallam Ibrahim heard about the school, it had already made a name for itself. He sought for admission through his mentor Maibabban Daki Mariya who ensured that his admission was processed and that he was allowed to take the entrance examination along with other applicants. He passed the examination and was admitted into the law school to study Advanced Islamic Studies with emphasis on Sharia Legal System. Mallam Ibrahim was an enthusiastic student who also had the rare privilege of being fluent in the Arabic language which was the medium of instruction in the school. He got along very well with both his tutors and fellow students. Some of his tutors at that time included Sheikh Nur, Sheikh Bashir Al-Rayyah, Sheikh Awad, all of them Sudanese, and Mallam Aliyu Jos, a Nigerian. Mallam Musa from Bauchi, Mallam Zaki from Ilorin, Mallam Sabo Indabawa from Kano and Mallam Talba from Borno who became his close friend, and a frequent visitor to his house in Kano, were some of his mates in the school. Some of the senior students in the school then were Mallam Halliru Binji, Mallam Abuabakar Mahmud Gumi, Mallam Sambo and Mallam Baffa.

At the end of the course, Mallam Ibrahim Ahmad passed his exams with flying colours, and he proceeded to serve his mandatory tutelage as a court clerk. After this period, he became one of the youngest persons to be appointed a mufti, that is, an Assistant Alkali. His first posting was to Gaya. Before leaving Kano to take up his posting in Gaya, Mai Babban Daki Mariya took a step to cement her relationship with Mallam Ibrahim by giving the hand of her niece Hajara, Adamu's daughter, in marriage to him as his first wife. Hajara had been living with MaiBabban Daki since the death of her father.

According to Mallam Bashari, Umaru's elder brother and first son of Hajara, the reception Mallam Ibrahim got in Gaya was both elaborate and enthusiastic. Mallam Ibrahim was presented to the late Sarkin Gaya, Mallam Abubakar Maisaje, by the emir's messenger (Yaron Sarki). Sarkin Gaya was very pleased to receive him and he was given a fairly large house to stay in. He reported to the Alkalin Gaya, late Mallam Gidado, at that time. He moved to Gaya from Kano with his newly married wife, Hajara, and other members of his household'.

The Birthplace: Gaya

Gaya, where Umaru was born, was then a growing metropolis which was shedding the toga of a rural settlement and developing into one of the fastest growing towns in the Kano emirate. This was made possible by the advantage Gaya had as an important groundnut market. Groundnut was then one of the major cash crops that were being produced and promoted all over the North and was a vital foreign exchange earner not only for the Northern Nigerian Government but also for the farmers themselves. Gaya was also a major terminus on the highly lucrative trade route from Kano to Maiduguri through Azare and Potiskum.

Apart from that, Gaya people have always prided themselves to be the founders of Kano with the saying, *Daga Gaya aka yi Kano* (it is from Gaya that Kano was founded). This is a common saying that has been handed down from generation to generation till the present. This is because oral tradition revealed that Kano city was founded by people from Gaya who were out searching for iron-stone and charcoal until they eventually settled in the Gwauron-Dutse/Dala area, which grew rapidly into what is now Kano city. The Abagayawa, as they were called then, fought, defeated and subjugated other competing groups to produce the first line of Habe Dynasty of Kano.

Movement to Wudil

The stay of Umaru's family in Gaya was short-lived as his father was transferred to Wudil, some twenty-five kilometres towards Kano. His recollection of this phase of his life in Gaya is hazy as the family left the town when Umaru was barely five years old. At Wudil, the family moved into spacious quarters that was reserved for the Alkali and which was a walking distance from the home of the District Head. Such arrangements were typical in the Northern region where the houses and offices of those associated with the district or township administration were congregated in close proximity. It was therefore not unusual that at Wudil, the Alkali's house, the court, the prison, the dispensary, the schools and all other organs of the native authority were all within the calling distance of the District Head's residence.

Umaru spent a good part of his childhood in that environment. He recalled that they had 'a large compound with very spacious rooms. We had big parlors and spacious playgrounds. Outside the house, there was a large tree where, at night, we sat with the neighbours, especially those from the District Head's household, to tell folk stories. Life was quite peaceful and very interesting'.

Umaru's father enjoyed good and mutually beneficial relationships with all his neighbours, particularly the family of the District Head, Alhaji Muhammadu Dan Kadan Kano. The District Head was a simple man, articulate, hardworking, God-fearing, good-natured and also a highly respected community leader. Many of the District Head's children became Umaru's lifelong friends and associates. One of such is Shehu Mohammed, Magajin Rafin Kano, who was once Managing Director of the defunct Allied Bank and who has been Umaru's close associate since their Wudil days. Other relations from that household whom Umaru counts as friends today include Dan Kadan Kano, Dr. Bashir Ibrahim, and Mustapha Muhammed Dan Kadan.

As the family was settling down in Wudil, little Umaru lost his mother. He was not more than eight years old and he did not understand the implication of his loss. In any case, this sad reality was cushioned by the effusive care he enjoyed in the large household with his step-mothers, the other children, his own sisters and several other relations.

The Beginning of Western Education for Umaru

It was at Wudil that little Umaru went to school. Fortunately, his visionary and forward-looking father had grasped the real essence of western education and had made up his mind to give his growing family the opportunity to be properly educated. Alkali Ibrahim Ahmed was progress-minded and was well aware of the issues concerning child education at that time and as a result of this, he encouraged all his male children to go to school. When it was time for Umaru to begin his education, his father walked him to the nearby Wudil Primary School to register him as a fresh pupil. Wudil Primary School was the only primary school in the town then. It was located close to the Craft School and the Teacher Training College (TTC). The two institutions were famous and considered highly reputable institutions in the North then. The Craft School was established by the Northern Nigerian government to promote vocational and technical education and it produced a great number of skilled young men who later became engineers and technicians all over Northern Nigeria. The Teacher Training College was one of the oldest in the north and it contributed to the training of teaching personnel in the region. Its premises later formed the nucleus of Kano State University of Science and Technology.

Umaru's younger brothers, Aliyu, Matawallen Kano and Shehu, now a judge of the Sharia court became his contemporaries in the school later. He also had ready role models in his elder brother, Bashari, as well as his cousins, Habibu Aliyu and Bello Abubakar, who were already in institutions of higher learning by that time.

Umaru stayed in the primary school for only about three years, as his father was soon transferred to Kano city.

Movement to Kano

When the family finally moved to Kano, the homestead at 14 D/Zungura within the city became their permanent abode for a very long time. Their father was never transferred out of Kano until after his retirement from the

Judiciary when Emir Ado Bayero made him the District Head of Babura in the 1970s.

Kano City of the 1960s

The Kano city that Umaru's family moved into in the early sixties was a growing city that was bubbling with life and verve. It was a city that was very much dominated by its Emir, Sarkin Kano Muhammadu Sanusi, who was then overseeing the expansion and modernisation of the city during the period. The Emir's illustrious father, Sarki Abdullahi Bayero, who had reigned for a period of 28 years, laid the foundation of modern Kano. By the time he died in 1953, Kano was the largest city in Northern Nigeria in terms of population, second only to Ibadan in the southern part of the country. The city also housed the richest native authority in Nigeria with revenue earnings above £1m a month, which was a princely sum at that time and which was wisely utilised by the prudent and pragmatic Emir Abdullahi Bayero and his successor to give Kano city the modern infrastructure that was hardly available in many cities in Nigeria of the 1950s.

Kano city had a long history dating back to 10th century when it was a major centre of the Trans-Saharan Trade and it retained this commercial status until the 1950s with flourishing markets at Kantin Kwari, Kasuwar Kurmi and Sabon Gari. These popular markets were patronised widely by traders from all over the country, as well as from neighbouring countries and even beyond. The city had been a major railway terminus since 1912 and it also had an airport that had been in use even before the 1st World War. There was electricity and pipe-borne water supply within the city. There were permanent offices for the native authority, a magnificent emir's palace and an imposing central mosque whose unique architecture was made famous on a postcard at the time. A number of secondary schools, a teacher training centre, an Arabic and Islamic studies school and many primary schools dotted the landscape of the city.

Modern residential buildings had sprouted around the city, becoming prominent among the ancient mud buildings. Movement within and around the city was easy as the different parts were linked together by reasonably good and motorable network of roads. However, there were very few cars and a good majority of the people still moved about on foot, bicycles, donkeys, horses and carts.

Despite all the modern artefacts in the city, it still retained its remarkable old self. There were closely packed houses made of mud, separated only by narrow alleys serving as footpaths; many only wide enough to permit a horse, a donkey or a camel to pass, but definitely not a car. There were open sewers and drainages, ditches, and hundreds of burrow pits, large and small, dotting the expansive landscape, but despite all these traditional trappings, Kano was obviously a modern city in the making.

Socially and politically, the city was agog with activities, particularly from the 1950s. Nigeria was in the throes of independence and political activities were intensifying all over the country, especially between political parties jockeying for leadership at the regional and federal levels. Kano became an important hub and a melting pot of national politics due to its size and strategic location. The conservative Northern People Congress (NPC) and the more radical Northern Elements People Union (NEPU) fought to garner jurisdiction within Kano city.

Back to School

It was against these socio-economic and political backgrounds that little Umaru and his family got settled in Kano. The first task the father performed for the family was to enrol Umaru, his brothers and sisters in a school. Fortunately, there was the Gidan Makama Primary School which was a short distance away from the family home. Umaru was registered in the school to continue from where he stopped in Wudil. Kano, then, had many primary schools around the city with impressive pupil enrolments. This was a far cry from the earlier years when parents had to be coerced to send their wards to the new schools.

Life in the primary school was eventful for young Umaru. The school was not far away from his home and every morning he walked or rode his bike to school and whenever he was in a more adventurous mood, he would hitch a ride from a native authority (pick-up) vehicle plying the road. Umaru recalled that his primary school experience was both pleasurable and adventurous. The teachers were serious, well-trained and dedicated to their duties. The population of pupils was manageable and there was a good mix of indigenes and non-indigenes. They were pupils from all the tribes in the same class. There was neither discrimination nor segregation. There were also teachers from other parts of the country who contributed their quota to nurture and develop the young pupils.

In those days, primary school education was in two phases. Pupils spent a total of seven years in school; the first four years as junior primary and the latter three years as the senior primary. The Gidan Makama Primary School was in the junior category, ending in the fourth year. When Umaru completed his first four years, he and his colleagues were sent to Gwale Senior Primary School for the next three years.

In both Gidan Makama and Gwale, young Umaru made friends fast, and many of them have remained lifelong associates. Among them is Abba Abdullahi who was from Umaru's father's own household and was one year behind him in the primary school. Garba Imam was his classmate throughout his primary school days. So also were the late Jibrin Isa and equally the late brothers Abubakar and Umaru Babba Dan Agundi. Ibrahim Shekarau, who was Kano State Governor, and more recently, Minister of Education, was also Umaru's junior in the primary school.

Secondary School

At the completion of his primary school education in 1964, young Umaru sat for the mandatory common entrance examination for admission into secondary school. Those who were successful were invited for an interview to sort out their placements into the categories of schools available. Some of the older students were destined for teacher training and craft schools. Umaru was one of the successful ones and when he came for the interview, he was to be interviewed by none other but the highly principled and strict K. J. Beer, a Briton, who was then the principal of Provincial Government Secondary School, Kano. This school, which was later renamed Rumfa College, was then the best institution offering secondary school education in Kano.

Umaru was successful at the interview and was admitted into form one. He came into a school whose illustrious history dates back to 1927 when it started as

Kano Middle School, a preparatory institution that drew its students from the elementary schools in the Kano province to prepare them for entry into Katsina College, the premier northern institution then, which was later moved to Kaduna. The middle school was the only one of its type in Kano during that period. Everyone in the Kano province who later became a person of substance in life passed through Kano Middle School. This included two former military Heads of State, Generals Murtala Mohammed and Sani Abacha, former Federal Ministers late Muhammadu Inuwa Wada, late Yusuf Maitama Sule, late Shuaibu Kazaure, Balarabe Isma'il, the late Emir of Kano, Ado Bayero, and a host of ministers of the old Northern Nigerian Government, namely, late Sule Gaya, late Umaru Babura, late Abdullahi Maikano, late Tijjani Hashim, late Bello Makaman Kano, and late Madakin Kano, Shehu Ahmed.

The school assumed the status of a secondary school in 1954, and was accordingly renamed the Provincial Government Secondary School, Kano. Umaru joined the 1965 set. The school had just joined other secondary schools of its kind to jettison the six-year programme and embrace the five-year programme. Also, instead of the normal two streams of sixty students, Umaru found himself in a class of one hundred and twenty, spread over four streams. The school was modelled on the British Grammar Schools, with full boarding facilities. Half of the teachers were expatriates and the remainder Nigerian teachers were a good mix of the different tribes from all over the country.

Umaru recalled that the school had everything that made life easier and conducive for academic pursuits. The school was one of the biggest, well-equipped, adequately and well-funded institutions. It had a highly trained, disciplined, motivated teaching staff. The school had enough books, good food, excellent recreational facilities, clubs and societies for extra-curricular activities. It had a very good system of leadership; ranging from House Prefects to School Prefects and Class Monitors. It was quite an excellent and well-run school. The students also had money for upkeep to buy such items like milk, sugar and groundnuts to supplement their food. They had soap every week for the laundry and so many other luxuries. In fact, every aspect of the students' necessities was adequately provided.

Umaru got admitted into secondary school in 1965 at a time when the country was witnessing a whirlwind of political upheaval. The British colonialists had granted political independence in 1960, leaving the budding regional parties to fight for control of the affairs of the country. At independence, two regional parties, the Northern People Congress (NPC), led by the Sardauna, Sir Ahmadu Bello and the National Council of Nigerian Citizens (NCNC), led by the Owelle of Onitsha, Dr. Nnamdi Azikwe, had gone into an alliance to control the central government, leaving out Chief Obafemi Awolowo's Action Group (AG) and other parties, such as the Northern Elements Peoples Union (NEPU), led by late Aminu Kano and the United Middle Belt Congress (UMBC), led by Joseph Tarka, in opposition.

However, by 1965, the leader of the opposition, Obafemi Awolowo was already in jail for treasonable felony and the western part of the country where his supporters were dominant, was in crisis. The followers of Awolowo felt aggrieved at the turn of events and would not allow peace to reign in the region as they believed that the charges against their leader were trumped up as a calculated and well-orchestrated attempt to get rid of him. This development, together with other perceived grievances against the leadership, all culminated into a situation which made a section of the military decide to organise a bloody coup to arrest the ugly situation and correct perceived injustice. The decision of the military to intervene in politics forcefully resulted in the murder of many prominent political and military leaders from both northern and western parts of the country. 1966 bore those horrors and many more, including reprisal killings and counter coups all leading to the bloody civil war that started in 1967.

Umaru and his young colleagues were witnesses to all these untoward and gruesome happenings. The national crisis impacted their lives in many ways, but they were virtually insulated as the school did everything within its capacity to shield them away from its direct impact.

There was much to imbibe from college life that was both full time and routine in nature. A typical day in the school started with the ringing of the bell at 5.30am for subh prayers, cleaning the compound, breakfast and morning drills. Classes started at 7.30am, with breaks for meals, siesta and games, till roll call at 8.00pm and lights out at 10.00pm. There were general inspections on Fridays, followed by attendance at the central mosque in the city for the Juma'at prayer. Every Friday, staff and students paid the emir a courtesy visit in his palace to receive his royal blessings and gifts. The school had also many extra-curricular activities. Different sporting activities were encouraged and engaged in on a daily basis. Students were also encouraged to join or form social and religious associations so as to expose them to wider issues and enable them reach out beyond the narrow confines of their schools.

Young Umaru was very active in the Muslim Students Society of Nigeria (MSSN). The MSSN was established principally to create Islamic consciousness among students and make them proud to be Muslims. The students interacted at their various meetings and more importantly at the Islamic Vocation Courses (IVC). These courses were particularly convenient as they were held during holidays which students attended at no cost. They enjoyed free meals and listened to series of lectures on various aspects of Islam. It was during such interactions that Umaru met and formed lasting friendships with colleagues such as Dr. Usman Bugaje, Prof. Munzali Jibrin, Prof. Sheikh Abdullah, Dr. Ibrahim Sulaiman, late Prof. Tijjani Elmiskeen, late Hanif Baba Ahmed and late Shehu Ladan, many of whom were not even students of Provincial Government Secondary School Kano. All these school activities, academic and social, impacted positively on the students that participated in them. For Umaru, the impact is life-long as it has kept him on a straight trajectory at all times.

In 1969, he sat for the West African School Examination and was looking forward to joining the Higher School Certificate class in the following year which was then a requirement for entry into Nigerian universities. However, fate had other plans for him which would propel him into the university much earlier than he had planned.

Becoming A Graduate

Life in the Provincial Government Secondary School, Kano came to an abrupt end for Umaru in December

1969; and by a combination of propitious factors, he found himself as a student in the university the month after he left secondary school. The Ahmadu Bello University, Zaria (ABU), the only higher institution then in the northern part of the country offering university education, had concluded plans to begin a School of Basic Studies in the late 1960. It was acting on a request from the Interim Common Services Agency (ICSA) of the northern states which was becoming concerned that only a limited number of its young and capable secondary school leavers were benefitting from university education. That was worrisome as it was slowing down the growth of the needed indigenous high-level manpower required for rapid development and for correcting the age-old imbalance in educational opportunities existing between the northern states and other parts of the country.

The Ahmadu Bello University had to come up with an ingenious solution that would not compromise standards and, at the same time, deal with the situation at hand. By this providential arrangement, Umaru found himself among the pioneer beneficiaries of this unique experiment when he joined the first set for a 5-term course which started in January 1970 and ended in July 1971. The year, 1970, was a watershed in Nigeria's history as the civil war that had run for three years was brought to an end early that year. At the end of the war, government funds was then channelled to reconstruction of infrastructure, education and other aspects of economic development. It was an opportunity for the northern states to focus on its only university, boost its student population and generally raise its standard. One of the ways was stating the School of Basic Studies (SBS).

The advantage of being a university student for Umaru that early was that, even though the students of the School of Basic Studies were pre-degree students, they became bona fide members of the university community. They benefitted from the excellent facilities available to prepare them for full university academic life. The School of Basic Studies was brand new in every aspect, from the buildings, facilities to their teachers. The pioneer principal was David Jester, a very serious and determined personality who was also an Anglican priest from the United States of America. And as ABU was experimenting with the American semester model, his appointment was justified, as putting the right peg in the right hole. He was later succeeded by Dr. A. K. Maduagbon and subsequently, Dr. Angulu.

It was obvious that Umaru had all the support of the family to seek for university education which could only be sought outside Kano. Even as a boy, he was used to travelling and mingling with other people from other states. His membership of the Muslim Students Society had afforded him the opportunity to travel to nearby towns of Katsina, Kaduna and other parts of the north. His father, though firmly rooted in Kano, had also travelled widely and in the course of working had met and interacted with other judges from other states of the north. Consequently, leaving Kano for Zaria was nothing out of the ordinary for Umaru.

At Zaria, Umaru had no problem settling down to university life. His integration into university life was total and all-embracing. He was allocated a room in one of the university halls of residence and had the privilege to share the room with a regular, full-time second year undergraduate student of the university. Most of the

School of Basic Studies students had full scholarship from their various state governments. Kano State Government was particularly generous as the scholarship covered both academic and living expenses of the student on campus. Umaru and his colleagues who were students on scholarship had the rare opportunity to face their studies squarely without the weight of financial encumbrances on them or their parents.

There were many other benefits Umaru and other SBS students enjoyed as members of the university community. They were mostly lectured by tutors in the regular university system and could relate to them accordingly. They had access to the wise counsel of many famous tutors in the university by attending their public lectures, debates and other academic activities. Umaru particularly enjoyed lectures and debates held in the university circuit by radical lecturers like Dr. Patrick Wilmot, late Dr. Bala Usman, late Dr. Ibrahim Tahir, late Prof. James O'Connell and others.

The facilities on the ABU campus were top-rated and first-class. Teaching facilities were adequate and ultra-modern. Umaru found the lecture halls adequate for the small classes and convenient for close interaction with the tutors. Apart from the regular lecture periods, there was provision for tutorial classes where small groups of students could engage in debating issues among themselves and with their lecturers. There were well-stocked libraries with old and new issues of publications and journals. Students could choose to use the main Kashim Ibrahim library or the smaller departmental libraries. The SBS had its own well-stocked library as well.

The residential halls were adequate and rooms were mostly shared by two students. The halls had good dining facilities and students were well-fed. Students had access to a recreation room with a television set, a radio, a table tennis and other gaming facilities. Sporting facilities were on ground for virtually all the games such as football, hockey, basketball, volleyball, squash and fives.

As members of the university community, Umaru and his mates in the SBS were brought into the mainstream of all the social activities on the campus. They could join and participate in the registered social clubs and the Students' Union. Umaru was active on the two fronts. He actively participated in many of the social clubs. The prominent social clubs then were Alpha, the Vandella and the Rainbow clubs. Subscription were paid to join to hold all sorts of social events and parties and in the process students mixed and interacted with other students from different parts of the country. He also remained active in the MSS and continued to attend the IVCs and other activities. He was also active in the Kano State Students Association which was instrumental in the management of affairs of the students' scholarship and other welfare matters.

What Umaru enjoyed most was his active participation in student unionism. He became a member of the Students Representative Assembly (SRA) very early on his arrival on campus. That was the parliament run by the students to debate their welfare issues and even engage themselves on wider issues dealing with the society in general. Tom Ikimi, Bello Halliru, Wakawa and Isa Mohammed Argungu (whom the SRA impeached in controversial circumstances) were some of the students' union presidents during Umaru's stay in the university.

He recalled that the impeachment of the President of the Students Union was unprecedented in the history of student unionism in Nigeria. The circumstances surrounding the impeachment had to do with the announcement by the military Head of State then, General Yakubu Gowon, to initiate the National Youth Service Scheme (NYSC) programme to hold in the period of one year between graduation and the beginning of the working life for Nigerian graduates. Government would pay a stipend to the graduates on the scheme who would be required to live and work in a state away from their state of origin. Students kicked against the idea vehemently due to the fact most students were always eager to start work immediately, earn a salary and settle down. The SRA in ABU met to condemn the proposal. However, for some inexplicable reasons, the President of the Student Union, Isa Mohammed Argungu, went to Kaduna to give a press conference supporting the NYSC proposal without the approval or the support of the general student body. Umaru recalled that even before the President returned to Zaria, he and three other colleagues namely Sani Kalgo, now a member of the House of Representatives, late Ma'eka Mohammed and late Tijjani Isma were so incensed that they mobilised and obtained signatures of the majority members of members of the SRA to impeach the President.

NYSC in Rivers State

Umaru graduated in June 1974 and was enlisted to embark on the mandatory one-year National Youth Service Corps (NYSC) scheme in Rivers State. The scheme as mentioned earlier was started by General Yakubu Gowon, Nigeria's military ruler, as one of his post-civil war measures to reconstruct, reconcile and rebuild the country. A category of Nigerian youth graduating from universities were to be compulsorily deployed to serve in states other than their own, for a period of one year, so as to inculcate in them the spirit of selfless service to the community and to inculcate the spirit of oneness and brotherhood of all Nigerians, irrespective of their ethnic, cultural, social or religious background. It was designed to be a gap year of sorts for the fresh graduate to travel, live and be integrated into another Nigerian community away from his own. This is to foster the knowledge and understanding of its customs and traditions, as well as its potentials and problems.

The graduates who participated in the first batch of the scheme in 1973 were deployed to serve as teachers in colleges, some as technical supervisors on construction sites and many as responsible officers in federal, states and local government offices. A substantial number also served in private companies.

Umaru's travel experiences as a youth had amply prepared him for what he was to expect during the service year. He had widely travelled during his secondary school days. And in the university as an activist in the Students Union, he had the opportunity to actively engage in the activities of the larger National Association of Nigerian Students (NANS) which took him many times to different university campuses across the country. He recalled that in their second year, they had organised a 'know your country' tour for fifty to sixty Ahmadu Bello University students. The students had taken off in two buses from Zaria through Gboko, Otukpo, Enugu, Nsukka, and Benin. They always stayed on the university campus available. Wherever they went, they would spend a few days on the campus and as it was a NANS initiative, they collaborated and mingled with the students, saw the town and the people. From Benin, they drove to the Akoka campus of the University of Lagos, then to the University of Ife and ended up at the University of Ibadan before going back to Zaria.

The trip afforded the students the rare opportunity to see the country at close range, especially after the civil war which ended in 1970. Wherever they went, particularly the eastern part of the country which had been the theatre of the civil war, they saw dwellings pockmarked by rampaging bullets everywhere from Enugu to Nsukka and even Ore, the areas where the fiercest of the battles took place. It was an eye opener for them to see the difficulties of nation building and it prepared them on graduation for their postings to other parts of the country. In due course, the NYSC postings were released and Umaru found that he had been posted to Port Harcourt, the capital of Rivers state, for his youth service.

Port Harcourt

When he arrived in Port Harcourt in August 1974, he was welcomed to a city that was still recovering from the tell-tale signs of the savagery of the civil war. He could see bullet-ridden buildings around a population showing signs of brutalising fatigue as a result of the psychologically disorientating stresses of the civil war. Of course he also found a flickering of social and economic revival as the state government (which was created in 1967, in the nick of the break-out of the war, but could barely take-off due to the halting challenges of the civil war) had by 1974 started to settle down to government business. Its offices have started to spread and there were signs of government activities all over the place. However, those who knew Port Harcourt in its earlier days would tell you that it had never been so down on its knees. In its heydays in the mid-sixties, it was known as "the Garden City", not only for its aquatic splendour and environmental beauty but also for the limitless business opportunities and economic advantages it afforded the daring and adventurous persons.

Port Harcourt, a relatively young city like Jos, Maiduguri, Kaduna and Enugu, was founded by the British colonialists in 1912. It was created to serve as a port for the export of coal from the Enugu coal-fields. Its location was strategic because of a natural deep water harbour on the Bonny River. The sprawling city was named after Viscount Lewis Harcourt, the then British Secretary of State for the Colonies (1910-15). In addition to its physical advantage, the area had the additional advantage of being sparsely inhabited by fishing folk and was not under the jurisdiction of any meddlesome traditional leaders.

The discovery of oil in the surrounding delta in the 1950s defined the future of the growing city of Port Harcourt. As the first shipment of Nigerian crude left the city in 1958, it became primarily an oil city. Its port grew quickly and after Lagos, it became the second busiest and largest city in the country, taking away business from the pre-colonial ports of Calabar, Brass and Bonny Islands. Being a new city, it attracted people in large numbers from other parts of the country and across the world. The civil war put a stop to that phenomenal growth as Port Harcourt became one of the first casualties of the civil war.

Life in Port Harcourt

When Umaru reported at Rivers State, he was directed to the NYSC camp then at Alu village, a few kilometers away from Port Harcourt. Together with colleagues from all over the country, they were kept in the NYSC camp, trained and drilled, before they were dispatched to their places of primary assignment. Umaru was sent to Pivotal Teachers Training College in Port Harcourt. The institution was established to produce large number of teachers in a short time to handle the explosion of pupils in primary schools after the introduction of universal primary education scheme. The college was newly created and packaged with students and staff and was to be domiciled at Premanebri, a town in the riverine area, away from Port Harcourt. However, on inspection it turned out that the facilities in Premanebri were not ready for a college of that magnitude. Therefore the college remained in Port Harcourt but was accommodated in another college called Stella-Maris Secondary School. They worked out a convenient shift system whereby students of Stella-Maris Secondary School attended the school in the morning and afternoon, while the students of Pivotal Teachers Training College used the same premises in the evenings.

Umaru was designated the Vice-Principal of Pivotal Teachers Training College and in due course became also the de-facto Principal because Chief A. K. Bob Manuel, the substantive Principal was usually away from the school on assignments. The Principal was running other homes in far-away Buguma and Degema, including the one in Port Harcourt, and would only be in the school a few days a week. The rest of the time he left the school in the safe hands of Umaru who worked diligently to get the school running well.

Umaru had a good time running the school. Besides the administrative duties which were hectic and demanding; he also taught the subject of African History, an activity he enjoyed tremendously. He had taken history as a subject in secondary school and he found it interesting having to go back to his text to read widely so as to prepare to give interactive and stimulating lectures to his students.

In running the school, he was fortunate that most of the teachers were his colleagues in the NYSC, many of whom he recruited himself and who helped a great deal to make the job pleasurable for him. They all had a decent accommodation at No.10 Bishop Johnson Street. Each one of them had a room to himself and they shared common facilities such as toilet and kitchen. Many of those who shared the house with Umaru were from Ahmadu Bello University, Zaria, but there were others from Ife, Ibadan, Nsukka and Lagos. Staying together was an experience that bonded them to become good friends for many years to come.

He also seized the opportunity of his stay in Rivers State to embark on an extensive tour, particularly of the riverine areas, many times going around Akassa, Brass, Nembe, Degema, Buguma and Abomina. He even went to see those places where ships were loaded with crude for export. In all these travels in the riverine areas, he was always baffled by the large number of other Nigerians, especially from his own part of the country who have settled and made these places their homes. Many had intermarried with the locals and had even attained a considerable social eminence within the communities.

The service year soon ran its full course and Umaru prepared to return home to Kano. By now, he had been won over to the overwhelming benefits of the NYSC. It should be remembered that he was among the student union leaders who were vociferous against the scheme when it was muted in 1972. He could not regret his actions as such because that was the consensus of the student bodies in all the universities then. However, in retrospect, he had a nagging feeling that the student bodies were bought over by their seniors who were due to graduate in June 1973. The seniors who were to be the first set of the scheme naturally kicked against it because they were anxiously waiting to graduate, take up gainful employment and lead a good life. They were anxious to buy their own cars and houses and start families. Obviously, they regarded the NYSC as an unnecessary intrusion and diversion and they did everything they could to forestall it. But as fate would have it, Umaru had an exciting and rewarding experience in Port Harcourt. He also experienced a good tutelage on the challenges of leadership because as a very young man, he was saddled with running an equally young institution, a college with the population of about 500 students and 30 teachers. The fact that he rose to the challenges magnificently was an indication of the leadership qualities he had even at that time.

CHAPTER TWO

THE KANO STATE CIVIL SERVICE

Beginnings in Kano State Civil Service

The other half of the nineteen seventies were indeed very traumatic for civil administration at all levels in Nigeria. A military coup had taken place in July 1975 which ousted General Yakubu Gowon, Nigeria's leader since 1966, spearheaded by his own lieutenants who had lost patience with his approach and handling of the pervasive cases of corruption and the general slow pace of development of the country.

The new rulers, led by General Murtala Mohammed, were just settling into office in Lagos, the federal capital territory, when Umaru joined the civil service in Kano State in August 1975 as an Administrative Officer and was posted to the seat of the government in the cabinet office of the Military Governor. The new governor, Lt. Col. Sani Bello, had assumed duties and typical of the crop of leaders then, there was palpable hurry to get things done. To start with, the entire political leadership of the previous regime was sacked and replaced with a new set of commissioners to form the State Executive

Council. Attention was then turned to the civil service to purge it of what the government felt were 'corrupt and indolent' elements. This meant that there was a sweeping and wholesale dismissal and/or retirement of top officials of the civil service.

Dismissing the political leadership was easy as the guidelines to their appointments were flexible. However, to succeed in getting rid of civil servants required a different manner of approach. The civil service in Nigeria was modelled after the British with laid down rules governing appointments and dismissals. These rules and regulations were codified in a book then referred to as General Orders. The G.O., as it was popularly called, never envisaged a situation of mass retirements and dismissals of civil servants without recourse to the rules and regulations written in the book. The exercise of purging the civil service that took place in Kano as well as in all the other states of the federation was hurriedly done under a specially promulgated decree which could not be challenged in any court of law in the country.

There were celebrations in many quarters for the mass purge just as there was anguish in many others. The cause for anguish in many cases was probably because those purged felt they were unjustly victimised. It was a period of great anxiety, anger and tension as those who were aggrieved kept writing petitions to the Military Governor for restitution, who in turn brought all these matters before the Executive Council for deliberations. The first few months Umaru spent in the cabinet office saw him witnessing all these deliberations in the council, as regards the retirement and dismissal of civil servants.

However, the most challenging aspect of the cabinet duties then were having to set up various probe panels to properly investigate the regime that was overthrown during the military coup. The new rulers reasoned that it was only by digging into the past, dredging up the damage that was done and meting out the appropriate punishment to those found to be responsible that the future of the country can be secured. In Kano, the Military Governor followed the footsteps of the federal government and other states to institute a number of probe panels to investigate the ousted regime.

Probing the Ousted Government

The first probe panel to start in Kano was the Wheeler Commission. The commission, which was headed by Justice A.W.E. Wheeler, looked into major contracts and other transactions of the previous administration. Most of these projects were channelled through and undertaken by the Ministry of Works. Therefore, when the Wheeler Commission began its work amidst intense publicity, scrutinising the execution of major contracts, probing the delays and the inevitable contract variations that followed; there was palpable tension and anxiety among the civil servants who participated. The affected civil servants were embittered by this treatment because they felt that they had given genuine leadership to matters pertaining to the initiation and general execution of these contracts. Whether it was the issue of setting up schools, hospitals, construction of highways or the provision of water supply to towns and villages, these civil servants felt they had done their best with the meagre resources available and that the variations were justified.

They stood no chance as the mood of the nation was not favourable to them. There was a generally held belief that the increased oil revenues accruing to the nation had been mismanaged and those at the helm of affairs must suffer the consequences of their actions and/or inactions. When the Wheeler Commission completed and submitted its findings, it was deliberated upon extensively in the Executive Council and finally, a White Paper was issued which vilified and punished many in the top leadership of the last regime.

The second one was the Ali Alhakeem Committee which examined the performances of all the Kano State Government parastatals, agencies and all other companies in the country where the state had the majority holdings. The mandates of sixteen Kano State Government organisations as well as seventeen companies where the state had majority holding were examined along with their responsibilities, key performances and their resources. The committee then worked out the justification for retaining, scrapping, privatising or auctioning them. They worked out a grading system for the government agencies based on their mandates, resources, expected deliverables and even determined the kind of quality its personnel needed, especially at the top echelon.

Ali Alhakeem did a very thorough and professional job. The membership of his committee comprised some of the best brains among Kano indigenes in the financial service industry who brought their expertise to bear on the outcome of the report. The white paper that emanated from the Alhakeem report made it possible for Kano State Government to reorganise its companies and agencies, positioned them properly and worked out a durable scheme of investment for them through the Kano State Investment Company or the Northern Nigerian Development Corporation (NNDC) and its various affiliates.

The third panel of enquiry had to do with looking into funds that were raised during the previous regime to alleviate the hardship caused by the drought that devastated Kano and much of West Africa in the early 1970s. There was a nationwide committee initiated by the Federal Government under the leadership of Babatunde Jose, Chairman of the *Daily Times*, to raise funds for all the victims of the drought in the country. Kano State Government also inaugurated a similar fund raising committee under the late Uba Ringim and in the process a huge sum of money was raised. There were allegations of mismanagement against the committee and naturally the new governor decided to look into the matter. This enquiry and its outcome also generated a lot of tension and anxiety at the State Executive Council because some members felt that decisions taken against some senior administrative staff were harsh and unjust.

These enquiries and many that followed were an eye opener for Umaru who was then at the threshold of his career. He was at the vantage position to observe the assemblage of the members of the committees of enquiries. He was responsible for drawing up their terms of references, sending them their letters of appointment and arranging for them to be sworn in. He was part of the team that arranged logistics for them and generally kept a tab on their activities. Whenever the committees complete their assignments, their first port of call would be the cabinet office to submit their report, which would be processed and put before the Executive Council for deliberations and eventual decisions. Umaru and his colleagues prepared the White Paper and followed through with the implementation of the decisions.

The enquiries and their aftermaths were a defining feature of the late 1970s which made and destroyed the careers of some top civil servants and politicians alike. As the military regime wound down its activities towards the end of 1978 and was getting ready for the handover to civilians in 1979, the decisions of these enquiries became ready tools for the authorities to decide on who would run for elections into public office and who would not.

The Family – The Rock

A few years after settling down in Kano and taking a job with the state government, it became necessary for Umaru like all young men of his ilk to start a family. Fortunately, he met his future wife, Alawiyya Fatima Kuliya Umar, at a friend's wedding. They found out that their families had always been close. They both share the same backgrounds having come from learned families. Both their parents were Shari'a court judges and have known each other for long. Umaru had also known many of her relations right from secondary school. He was acquainted with her uncle, Gidado Mukhtar, who worked in the National Universities Commission and was also a Director in AP (Africa Petroleum). Umaru also knew another uncle, Sarki Mukhtar, who was a General in the Nigerian Army and over the years became a State Governor, Ambassador and National Security Adviser. With all these links in place, it was therefore easy for the families to accept the relationship.

When the marriage took place in August 1978, Umaru was just 28 and his bride Alawiyya was still a student of Chemistry in the Bayero University.

Today, she still maintains that girlish charm that stole Umaru's heart back then. According to Umaru, she still remains the same girl that he had known almost right from the cradle. He spoke lovingly about her total commitment and focus, her total faith in God and her academic brilliance. Indeed, she was able to combine pursuing a degree in Chemistry at a tender age, thereafter a Master's Degree and managing the home front made up of seven successful children plus her husband, together with her own career.

At graduation and after the mandatory NYSC, she worked as a chemistry teacher in the Kano State College of Arts and Remedial Studies (CAS). And when the family moved to Lagos, she was able to secure appointment with the National Directorate of Employment (NDE) and rose by dint of hard-work and perseverance to the position of Director.

She retired as a Director from the National Directorate of Employment (NDE) and now runs an educational institution of her own. She is also a successful poultry farmer, having being in the business of raising chicken for many years.

With a twinkle in her eyes, she spoke about her husband and how great he is as a husband, helper and father. She attested to the fact that one of the things that had helped her marriage immensely was her husband's natural disposition. According to her, "Living with him is the easiest thing one can think of. It is an uncommon experience and favour from Allah." They have been married for forty years and she found it difficult to recall an instance when he had raised his voice when he was angry at her or the kids. She said that Umaru never allowed anything to bother him. In fact, to her, he has an innate shock absorber with the way he shrugged off tension and challenges.

Their marriage has been successful also because of the residual chemistry and unwavering belief in Allah. In her opinion, the live wire of their marriage is having a symbiotic relationship which bonded them into one indivisible unit. According to her, this has rubbed off on the marriages of their children too. She said that with the spirit of love, patience and understanding, there was nothing that could not be surmounted in a marriage.

The family is blessed with seven children who have all gone through guidance and tutelage in various schools and are now getting on well in their various endeavours. The first child of the family, Laila Umaru, was born in 1979. She read Medicine in the University of Maiduguri and later got a Master's Degree in Public Health from the Sheffield University. She is presently engaged in the Primary Health Care unit of Federal Ministry of Health. She is married with two kids.

The second child Ibrahim Mu'azzamu Umaru was born in 1981. He schooled in the Airforce Command Secondary School and read Mechatronics Engineering in the University of Manchester and also acquired a Master's Degree from Loughborough University. He is now running a consulting and construction company. He is also into mining in the Jos Plateau. He is married with three children.

Aliyu Umaru, the third child was born in 1985. He attended Adesoye College, Offa and read Communication and Computing Engineering in Manchester University, United Kingdom. He now runs an ICT consulting and contracting company. He is also into farming and processing of crops.

The fourth child (Aliyu's twin) is Aliya Umaru who also attended Adesoye College where she had a very brilliant career and leadership position as the school Head Girl. She read Medicine in Manchester University, United Kingdom. She is now a Senior Registrar in a Southampton Hospital and is married with three children.

Mohammed Umaru the fifth child was born in 1989. He was a pioneer student of the Nigerian Turkish College, Kano. He read Civil Engineering in the University of Cairo and received a Master's Degree from Cardiff University. He is now a Facility Manager in the Central Bank of Nigeria (CBN).

Hafsat Umaru, the sixth child was born in 1991 in Lagos. She attended Airforce Primary School, Lagos and Adesoye College, Offa. She read Economics in the University of Hull, United Kingdom and also received a Master's Degree in Islamic Finance from Durham University. She is now married with two children and is running a business consultancy and a tailoring boutique in Kano.

Husna Umaru is the last born in the family. She was born in 1995 and attended Adesoye College Offa. She was the Head Girl of the school and lead speaker of the school debate team as well as the Amirah of the Muslim society. She read Architectural Technology in Liverpool John Moores University where she finished with a First Class Degree in 2016 and was celebrated for finishing with a perfect 5.0 GPA. She also has a Master's Degree in Design from Instituto Marangoni, Milano. She is currently undergoing the one-year compulsory National Youth Service Corps.

The Abubakar Rimi Era

Those were curiously interesting times indeed. As the 1970s were coming to an end, events were occurring all over the country at a frenetic pace. The military regime after losing its leader, General Murtala Mohammed, in an attempted coup in February 1976, was set on a course of transferring the reins of power to civilians. A detailed transition programme had been announced by the new military strongman, General Olusegun Obasanjo, leading to a formal handover to a democratically elected government on 1st October, 1979.

Umaru, after securing his first two promotions, had been posted from the cabinet office to the political department of the Secretary to the State Government. At that time, the SSG was the late Isa Gambo Dutse, but Umaru reported directly to Sule Yahaya Hamma who was the Under Secretary in the political department. The Military Governor, Lt. Col. Sani Bello, had also been redeployed and Aboi Shekari, an Airforce Officer, had taken over with a new title of Military Administrator, to oversee the transition to a civilian administration.

Activities in the new posting were happening at a fast pace in the cabinet office. Umaru was the Senior Assistant Secretary (Political), and his duties included liaising with the new political associations that had been registered as political parties in 1978 by the military regime as part of the preparations for civilian rule in the coming year, 1979. He had the rare opportunity to learn a great deal from monitoring the formation of political associations that in a short while metamorphosed into political parties. He keenly followed the constitutional debate that was initiated by the military government as a prelude to the final processes of handing over power to civilians. His schedule also brought him closer to the state electoral body working together to ensure that all the processes and materials for the elections were in place.

Perhaps what he found most interesting was witnessing the political maneuvers which culminated in the formation of the National Party of Nigeria (NPN) and the People Redemption Party (PRP), the two political parties that became dominant in the state. The emergence of gubernatorial candidates to lead the political parties was particularly raucous. That was more so in the PRP because all indications pointed to the fact that the party would be the first civilian administration in the state as Mallam Aminu Kano, one of the most charismatic and popular politician in the country, led the party. Initially, Engr. Salihi Iliyasu was nominated as the gubernatorial candidate of the PRP, but he had issues with his tax papers and the party had to withdraw him. Another snag was that one of the panels of enquiries that looked into the affairs of the ousted regime when Engr. Salihi Iliyasu was Permanent Secretary, Ministry of Works, had indicted him of some malpractices. He felt betrayed and unjustly treated by those he regarded as his professional colleagues. He was even appointed as a Commissioner in the Executive Council under Lt. Col. Sani Bello, but he protested against the appointment and left in a huff. At that point in time, one could discern disagreements and divergences creeping in even at the level of the State Executive Council when holding deliberations on the findings and recommendations of the enquiries panels. Many members of the Executive Council left for the new political parties; some to NPN, others to PRP.

The Rimi Administration

As fate would have it, Abubakar Rimi emerged as gubernatorial candidate of the PRP and won the election. He also had a comfortable majority in the State House of Assembly to work with. Governor Rimi appointed Sule Yahaya Hamma as Secretary to the Government. Sule Yahaya Hamma, Umaru's boss in the Political Department was obviously a good choice, because he had his immense knowledge and experience in governance, and of course, he had been at the right place at the right time.

Abubakar Rimi took to the administration of the state like a duck to water. He was an accomplished civil servant who also had experience as a diplomat. He came to government with great zeal and desire to serve the people and deliver democratic dividends in form of programmes and policies towards boosting the social and economic well-being of the state. He carefully selected a good team of commissioners to form the nucleus of his vibrant executive council. He also showed acute good sense in his selection of permanent secretaries and heads of parastatals who were highly skilled, experienced and committed technocrats to help him administer the state successfully. Rimi made sure that they had all the resources to work with and he allowed them absolute powers to deal with situations in their different agencies and parastatals. Umaru recalled the non-interference posture of the governor in the day to day running of its agencies. Once a mandate was given with its budget, resources and limits, there was no breathing down the neck unless something went clearly wrong, and of course, that was dealt with precision.

Those who had the knowledge of what transpired during that period lauded Rimi's dexterous handling of his executive council. Even though Umaru had left the secretariat of the executive council at the eve of the civilian administration, he learnt from his colleagues that

Rimi was a liberal chairman of council who allowed open discussions and debates on issues before taking a decision. The open and unrestrained input into the decision making process together with his non-interference policy in the day to day running of the agencies would explain the monumental achievements Rimi recorded in the area of provision of basic amenities such as water supply, schools, hospitals and rural electrification projects.

Rimi's Radical Moves

However, Governor Abubakar Rimi faced an uphill task governing the state right from the first day of his administration. He made radical moves and introduced novel measures aimed at upturning the traditional authorities in the state and at the same time, giving psychological satisfaction to the generality of the populace. Rimi's big moves included the abolition of head and cattle tax, banning the use of helmets for motorcycle riders and splitting Kano into Auyo, Gaya, Rano emirates and appointing emirs to rule them.

1980 was a tough year for the Rimi administration in Kano State. Besides the fresh difficulties of conducting government business in an environment that was used to military administration, Rimi faced immense pressures caused by the radical measures he initiated on assumption of office. In addition to these, he had problems within his political party, the People Redemption Party (PRP), where different factions seemed to have emerged. Actually, the PRP was a party that was ideologically to the left in the Nigerian political spectrum and typical of most large political parties factional cleavages tend to crop up within as it did in the PRP. Rimi and some of his colleagues, along with Balarabe Musa, the Kaduna State

Governor, represented the more radical face of the PRP referred to in the Kano local parlance as *'yan santsi'*, that is, those that have slipped away from the mainstream. The less radical group in the party called *'yan tabo'*, are those that were firmly rooted within the mainstream ideology of the party and coalesced around the national leader of the party, Mallam Aminu Kano. This meant a divided house for the Rimi administration which added political dichotomy to the other problems of those radical measures highlighted.

To compound the problems facing the government, Governor Rimi instituted a commission of enquiry into land matters. This was a highly sensitive political matter which did not go down well with the traditional institutions and it would go on to have very serious repercussions and implications. Justice M. B. Layola, a justice of the high court, was appointed the Chairman of the commission of enquiry and Umaru acted as its Secretary together with other members, many of whom were notable professionals in their different professions and the other appointees were from the State House of Assembly. As the Secretary of the commission, Umaru provided all the secretarial logistics for the one year during which the commission undertook its assignment.

The commission toured all parts of Kano State (now Kano and Jigawa States) conducting public hearing with thousands of witnesses, examining numerous documents relating to land matters and looking into all sorts of complaints of either one individual or the other appropriating land without justification. It was a trying time for the elites of Kano as the enquiry seemed to set them against the masses. Even Mallam Aminu Kano was alleged to have appropriated land belonging to 'talakawa' in parts of Tudun Wada area and he had to engage the services of a legal practitioner to clear his name. Open accusations were also directed at the Emir of Kano including his district heads and many other notables. It was a very tense period in the state. The kitchen cabinet of the Rimi administration did not help matters through their careless behaviour of discussing the enquiry's findings openly and hinting at the dire consequences coming to those who are likely to be indicted. What happened next was beyond anybody's expectations. When the committee submitted its report, there was an attempt to draft a White Paper. The government team, led by Dr. Bala Mohammed, a political adviser to Governor Rimi, had retreated to Tiga Dam to produce the White Paper when riots broke out in Kano. There were fears by some vested interests that the drastic actions that will follow the implementation of the White Paper would go against certain interests in the state. Expectedly, the riots resulted into monumental damage to the state; many government buildings were targeted, particularly the land registry in the Ministry of Lands, which was torched. Dr. Bala Mohammed's house was not spared and in the process, he was also gruesomely murdered.

Even while all these crises were on Rimi had to content with a very serious religious uprising. This was the 'Maitatsine' uprising that surfaced in 1981. A fiery Islamic religious preacher sought the support of his supporters to unleash a large scale insurgency against the state within Kano city. It was perhaps a most unfortunate and destabilising saga leading to a wholesale loss of lives. Fortunately, the Federal Government rose to the occasion by deploying a contingent of the Nigerian Army to crush the insurgency.

Secondment to WRECA

On the political front, more problems for the Rimi administration continued to rear their ugly heads and the division within the PRP exacerbated. This led to the open confrontation of the governor and his party leader, Mallam Aminu Kano. The party eventually broke up as a result of the irreconcilable differences in vested interests.

While all these were going on, Umaru continued to function within the office of the Secretary to the Government, headed by Sule Yahaya Hamma. He combined the busy schedules at the political desk with those of Secretary of many committees. At that point in time, he was heavily involved in the Layola Commission of Enquiry into Land Matters. Despite these busy schedules, Umaru craved new challenges.

It was about this time that a vacancy for the position of Secretary in the Kano State Water Resources and Engineering Construction Agency (WRECA) was advertised in 1980. The erstwhile Secretary of the agency, Bashir Dalhatu, had left to become the National Secretary of the National Party of Nigeria and WRECA had to put up an advertisement to fill the vacant position.

Umaru indicated his interest in the position of Secretary, WRECA by putting up an application for it. About half a dozen other candidates also indicated their interest. All of them, together with the person in acting capacity, were invited for an interview. Umaru emerged as the most suitable candidate at the interview and was offered the appointment along with his bosom friend, Ado Abdullahi, who was appointed Head of the Human Resources Department. However, it took Umaru close to a year to report to WRECA due to his unfinished assignment with the Justice Layola Commission of Enquiry into Land

Matters in Kano State. The fact that he occupied a very sensitive and strategic position as the Secretary of the commission prevented his sudden departure. Therefore, his assumption of duties at WRECA was delayed until a about year after he had been appointed.

Umaru came into WRECA when it was still a beehive of activities. It is on record that during the 1970s and 80s, WRECA was the most important agency of the Kano State Government, attracting a large chunk of the state budget. Governor Audu Bako, early in his administration, deemed it fit to carve out the water division of the Ministry of Works, incorporated it into an agency and charged it with the responsibility of harnessing the abundant water resources of the state. It took over all the resettlement and water supply schemes in the state. A Sri-Lankan engineer working with the Ministry of Works, Mr. Kalatunga, was appointed the pioneer Managing Director. After a few years of laying an excellent foundation for the agency, he was replaced with Engineer Magaji Abdullahi, as the first indigenous Managing Director. Magaji Abdullahi was also a staff of the water division of the Ministry of Works. WRECA is credited with building the Tiga, Bagauda, and all the other big dams all over Kano State and sinking hundreds of boreholes and wells. The dams also became sources of raw water for Kano municipality and its environs.

Umaru found WRECA to be a well-established and professionally-run organisation. It paraded highly skilled artisans, craftsmen and engineers; many of whom were sourced from polytechnics around the country. There were also a number of professionals in soil engineering, water engineering and geology who came from Hungary and Philippines. WRECA was privileged to have the kind of leadership it had at the time. Perhaps that was why it escaped the unfortunate controversies on land compensation resulting in loss of lives as it happened in other water projects such as Bakolori Dam in Sokoto State. The extension service unit of WRECA was well-known and well-grounded among the people. They made extensive consultations with the villagers, their ward heads and traditional rulers at all times before acquiring the land. The extension unit was also equipped with up-to-date survey equipment and maps to facilitate assessment of farmlands, economic trees, houses and all other structures before any move was made to shift villagers and resettle them. If villagers were to be moved, WRECA was always ready to give them alternative land, build houses for them where necessary and pay them compensations. There was never any violent resistance or communal clash over land matters.

WRECA placed a great premium on manpower development. It sent its workforce in batches to various universities and polytechnics in the United Kingdom for postgraduate degrees in various fields. One of WRECA's staff who enjoyed this kind of gesture was Engineer Rabi'u Musa Kwankwaso who, after successfully acquiring a postgraduate qualification, returned to the organisation to work briefly before venturing into politics. He later clinched his party's ticket, secured a seat in the National Assembly and eventually became one of the Principal Officers there. He crowned his foray into politics by becoming the Governor of Kano State in 1999. After the first term, he was appointed Minister of Defense by President Obasanjo. Kwankwaso returned to contest and win in the Kano Gubernatorial Election of 2011 to clinch a second term.

Umaru stayed in WRECA till October 1983 when a change in the government necessitated him to return to the main stream of the civil service. However, as the Secretary of WRECA, he had a smooth time, with the exception of one incident that occurred towards the end of his tenure. Workers in WRECA embarked on an industrial action that shut down the entire water system of the state and this wreaked havoc, particularly on the water supply in Kano city, which caused a great embarrassment for the state government. The industrial action was, however, a culmination of major grievances towards the state government, particularly on the issue of austerity measures imposed across the state due to paucity of funds. WRECA was particularly hard-hit because the workers enjoyed a special agency allowance of fifty per cent of basic salary which the government was constrained to stop. They were the highest paid agency in the state and when these allowances were withdrawn, it did not go down well with the workers. They kept on agitating but the state government could not rescind the decision as the austerity measures were nation-wide. The WRECA workers were a sizeable proportion of the state work force. They had a good idea of their strength. They were strongly unionised, belonging to the Nigerian Labour Congress, which meant they could canvass for the support of other unions in case of disagreements with the state government.

Somehow, political maneuverings was introduced into the matter. It was an election year and the inter-party rivalry between NPN and PRP had started manifesting. Also, within the PRP itself the *'yan santsi'* and *'yan tabo'* dichotomy had caused deep division in the party. All these added considerable fuel to the workers' agitation in WRECA. Therefore, it could not have been a coincidence that when the workers decided to go a step further to hold a public protest, they did so on a particular day when Balarabe Musa, a stalwart of the *yan santsi* faction of the PRP, was returning to Nigeria through the Kano Airport after his self-exile. Balarabe Musa was impeached as Kaduna Governor and he flew out of the country to rest. He was returning to the country and Governor Rimi his close associate planned to receive him in a big way. It was a big embarrassment for the government because the workers shut down Kano city on that fateful Friday. The Managing Director of WRECA was out of town that day and Umaru, as second in command, was left to face the wrath of both the workers and the government. He had a very rough time with the workers when he went to make a direct appeal to them at the premises of Challawa. Umaru was almost lynched as the workers were not ready to be otherwise persuaded. They were thoroughly embattled. He had to escape when every effort failed to achieve the desired purpose. The same day, he was called to the Government House to face the State Security Council chaired by Governor Rimi to give a detailed explanation about the protest.

Becoming a Permanent Secretary

In the 1983 elections, Governor Abubakar Rimi lost the bid for a second term of office due to the intra-party feud that had engulfed his party, the Peoples Redemption Party (PRP). The party broke into two factions: the *Yan Tabo* and *Yan Santsi*. Unfortunately for Governor Rimi, his faction the *Yan Santsi* lost the favours of the national leader of the party, Mallam Aminu Kano. Abubakar Rimi left the party and in frustration joined the Nigerian Peoples Party (NPP). The NPP did not have much support in the far-northern states and Rimi joined it at a late hour and expectedly did not make any impact. Thus he lost the election to Senator Bakin Zuwo who rallied the *Yan Tabo* faction to win the election and become Governor. It was just tragic that after the Kaduna State Governor Abdulkadir Balarabe Musa, Rimi became the second prominent victim of the political crises within their party, the PRP.

The new Governor, Sabo Bakin Zuwo had hardly assumed office in October 1983 when there was a military coup in the country at the end of December. As was usual with such happenings all the elected governors, members of the National Assembly and all other political appointees were swept away by the powers of military decrees. The military government settled in power and quickly installed its own men as governors, ministers and chief executives of government corporations.

A new Military Governor, Air Commodore Hamza Abdullahi, had assumed duties in Kano and in the new appointments to run the affairs of the state, Umaru Ibrahim found himself being appointed a Permanent Secretary. Towards the end of 1983, Umaru's secondment to WRECA had expired and had returned to the main stream service in the state government and was posted to Ministry of Finance as Under-Secretary. He was there for just a few months when the new Military Governor decided to appoint a new crop of top public servants in January 1984.

One morning, all top officials were summoned to Government House to witness the swearing-in of Sadauki Abubakar Kura as the new Secretary to the Military Government (SMG). During that period, there were no permanent secretaries, as all those in that category who served the previous regime had been compulsorily retired. Umaru, though an Under-Secretary was among the top civil servants invited to the government house for the occasion. After the main event of swearing-in of the new SMG, words went round to those gathered that new permanent secretaries would also be sworn-in. When the names of the newly appointed permanent secretaries were called out Umaru was stunned to hear his name.

It was only later that Umaru learnt that the Kano State Civil Service Commission had undertaken a painstaking background test of all the prospective permanent secretaries. The background investigations were done discretely to check qualification, experience, character, seniority and suitability. It was a combination of these factors that the Civil Service Commission then under the guidance of the Chairman, Isa Gambo Dutse, used to come up with the names of those fit and proper to occupy the offices of permanent secretary. It was a period when appointments to top position in the civil service were done purely on merit.

As soon as the ceremonies of swearing-in were concluded, the new permanent secretaries were assigned portfolios. Umaru found himself returning to his old haunts, as he was assigned the portfolio of Council Secretariat in the Cabinet Office and also state security matters in the Government house. He was also the youngest to be appointed. He was barely thirty-four years old and had worked for only ten years after graduation. However, he was lucky as a fresh graduate because his first assignment was in the Cabinet Secretariat which exposed him to the workings of government and the dynamics of governance. That was during the era of Colonel Sani Bello, the Governor who came in immediately after General Yakubu Gowon was overthrown in 1975. Umaru was privileged to work under some of the finest public servants in the country. The Secretary of the Government was Engr. Balarabe Isma'ila and some of Umaru's direct bosses were Abdulrahman Sambo and Muhammed Inuwa Saleh (MI Saleh). Another person he worked with and became very fond of as a mentor is Sule Yahaya Hamma. Both Umaru and Yahaya Hamma were contemporaries in secondary school as well as in the university, incidentally in the same Political Science Department and they found themselves in the Cabinet Office.

The later years of the 1970s were turbulent with investigations and enquiries of top officials of the previous Gowon regime. Umaru as a young administrative officer in the Cabinet Office was saddled with so many responsibilities in that direction. The atmosphere in the office was always volatile and the routine very challenging. He was there for the first two years before he decided to return to his alma mater, ABU, in the 1977/78 session to burnish his credentials with a Master's Degree in Public Administration. When he returned from Zaria, he was seconded to WRECA where he was exposed to different kinds of administrative and political challenges. And thereafter, when his secondment ended and on posting to ministry of finance, he experienced another kind of administrative experience working away from the Cabinet Office in the ministry.

As Permanent Secretary in the Cabinet Office, the job was challenging. Umaru said: "It was a 24-hour job. There were weekly Executive Council meetings. You have to prepare the memo, collate everything, distribute and share timely production of minutes. Sometimes, it was the extracts which you must distribute on time and as much as possible before the next meeting. And you have to get one or two feedbacks from agencies and ministries as a follow-up to what transpired. It was a challenging period. But one was inspired by the exemplary leadership."

For most of the period Umaru was Permanent Secretary, he was retained in the Cabinet Office which was a mark of regards to his competence and commitment to duty. He once spent a short period in the Ministry of Social Welfare but was promptly recalled to the Cabinet Office.

A Change of Turf: From Kano Civil Service to the Banking Sector

One day in 1988, Umaru Ibrahim was performing his normal official functions as Permanent Secretary in charge of Finance and Administration in the Governor's Office. His office was the live wire of the Governor's Office in charge of coordinating activities among the ministries, departments and agencies. On a typical day, Umaru Ibrahim would be at the centre of a flurry of activities; poring over volumes of paper work, attending to a horde of visitors from all walks of life, receiving and making phone calls to various functionaries of government, superintending over departmental affairs, attending meetings along with his boss, the Secretary to the State Government, and probably the Governor himself.

For a young man of Umaru's age, it was an exciting and fulfilling job, working within the very heartbeat of government. It was a highly demanding position that was full of various responsibilities and wide ranging frenetic activities. It was on one of those days in the office, in between these hectic activities, that Umaru Ibrahim received a phone call from Shehu Mohammed, a childhood friend of his, who was then serving in Lagos as one of the Executive Directors in the First Bank of Nigeria. What he heard from him that day would have a major impact on the trajectory of his career, and would eventually take him away from Kano to Lagos and also take him away from the civil service to the banking sector.

It was in the evening of that same day, and away from the hustle and bustle of the office in a more relaxed mood at home, that he was able to digest the information he got from Shehu Mohammed. The information he got was that the Central Bank of Nigeria, following in the footsteps of its kind in other parts of the world, had decided to create a deposit insurance agency to be headquartered in Lagos. The agency would function as a financial safety-net for all depositors in Nigerian banks so as to engender confidence and stability of the banking sector. This development arose as a fallout of the Structural Adjustment Programme (SAP) that was introduced by General Ibrahim Babangida, which greatly liberalised the banking and financial sector of the Nigerian economy. The programme made it possible for more banks to come into the system, but with the obvious possibilities of failures and the disastrous consequences it would have on the health of the economy. Inevitably, there had to be a deposit insurance system to ameliorate the effect of the situation when it happens. The newly established agency, named Nigeria Deposit Insurance Corporation was billed to start operations shortly and the apex bank was already recruiting all categories of staff for the new institution across the country. Shehu Mohammed also told Umaru that if he was interested, it was the right time for him to take a decision and make a quick move.

Umaru had not contemplated leaving the state government at that material time. The fact is that since his university days at Ahmadu Bello University, Zaria, where he was a Kano State Government scholarship student, he had looked forward to returning to Kano to serve the government and the people as a way of giving back to the society that had been generous to him. He willingly returned to join the government at the end of his mandatory National Youth Service in 1975. He was offered appointment as an Assistant Secretary, which he accepted and was posted to start work in the office of the Secretary to the Government. He rose rapidly through the ranks to the top position of a Permanent Secretary within a space of less than ten years in 1984. He had all but given his dues, because by 1989, he had served the state government for fourteen years, out of which he spent five years as Permanent Secretary in the Cabinet Office. The job was then becoming routine and drudging to him. Umaru, who was not averse to change, had always kept an open mind on the issue of changing to a fairly different but equally challenging job.

Fortunately, this opportunity coincided with a period when Kano State Government was vigorously encouraging its qualified and talented citizens to seek for appointments in the Federal Government institutions so as to redress the historical imbalance and afford the indigenes to take their rightful places among their compatriots. He knew, therefore, that the state government would not be a stumbling block if he decided to move to a federal establishment. As he had expected, he got a listening ear when he raised the matter with his boss, Sadauki Abubakar Kura, the Secretary to the State Government, who encouraged him to take the step whenever he finally decide to move.

He had to further make wider consultation among his family members and friends. He had to particularly consider that he was uprooting his family from their familiar surroundings in Kano to move to Lagos which at that time had a reputation of being a challenging place to live. Lagos, in 1989, still had the dual status as the federal capital territory and state capital, as well as being the commercial nerve center of the country. It was a densely-populated and congested city with attendant difficulties of transportation and accommodation. His wife, who was also a civil servant with Kano State Government, would have to find another job in Lagos. His young school-going children would have to be enrolled in other schools in Lagos. It was a difficult decision for him to take, but his destiny beckoned.

After considering all the extenuating factors, Umaru took a decision to join the Nigeria Deposit Insurance Corporation (NDIC). From that point on, events moved very fast. In due course, he received an invitation letter from the Central Bank of Nigeria to attend an interview in Lagos. Umaru recalled that, "Shehu Mohammed actually sent the invitation letter to me at home. I responded to the invitation and attended the interview in Lagos, which was chaired by Dr. Ayuba Musa, who was Deputy Director, Human Resources in the Central Bank of Nigeria. There was a panel of five people. I was interviewed among other candidates and by divine favour from Allah the Magnificent, I was successful. Obviously, I knew next to nothing about the NDIC. But luckily, Shehu Mohammed gave me a copy of the Decree establishing the NDIC at that time. I read it carefully and asked questions about it. Luckily again, our SMG in Kano State, Alhaji Sadauki Abubakar Kura, happened to be a seasoned banker and economist. So I told him that I had this invitation to attend an interview in NDIC and asked him a number of questions. He guided and educated me on a number of topics relating to banking and NDIC in particular, which really helped me a lot."

Umaru confidently went through the interview. After all, he had become familiar with the Decree establishing the NDIC after rigorous study of it and he had also reached out immediately to those acquaintances that were knowledgeable in banking matters to seek guidance before embarking on the trip to Lagos for the interview. Fortunately, he had also just returned from an advanced programme at the University of Oxford in the United Kingdom which gave him a great exposure and helped to broaden his knowledge of banking, finance and ICT. All these helped Umaru to have a smooth sail through the interview which was conducted by a committee chaired by Dr. Ayuba Musa. A letter of appointment was dispatched to him, giving him six months within which to tidy up his affairs and report for duty.

Before taking up the appointment, Umaru had to sort out a problem regarding the position he was offered by NDIC. He had been offered the position of Assistant Director which he considered below his status. He knew two of his colleagues who were offered the higher position of Deputy Director. One of the applicants was a Permanent Secretary from a small, rural state. Umaru was coming as a Permanent Secretary from the old Kano State which had one of the biggest, well-established and most successful civil services in the country, where he had worked for five years. He sought for an audience with the Governor of Central Bank, who also doubled as Chairman of NDIC Board of Directors, late Abdulkadir Ahmed to lay his complaint. He went to meet the Central Bank Governor in company of his friend, Shehu Mohammed. The Governor appreciated Umaru's grievance and he asked him to write a letter of appeal. In a matter of two weeks, Umaru got a new offer for the post of Deputy Director, which he promptly accepted and immediately started the process of disengagement from the Kano Civil Service. Umaru considers the prompt intervention of late Abdulkadir Ahmed as instrumental to making up his mind finally to join NDIC till the very present.

CHAPTER THREE

NIGERIA DEPOSIT INSURANCE CORPORATION (NDIC)

A New Beginning at NDIC

Umaru reported to the NDIC headquarters on 22nd March, 1989 in Lagos. The office, rented then, was on the 14th floor of the National Bank building on the ever busy Broad Street in the very heart of the business district of Lagos. Those were the pioneering days of the corporation. Every staff was fresh and newly appointed. Many of them came from the Central Bank of Nigeria. Late John U. Ebhodaghe, who was the pioneer Managing Director of NDIC, was at that time the Chief Bank Examiner (equivalent to Director now), Banking Supervision Department of the Central Bank. Actually it was in one of the units of his department in the Central Bank, the Financial Sector Development division, that the very idea of starting a deposit insurance scheme was hatched and carried out with the active support and approval of a visionary Governor of the Central Bank of Nigeria (CBN), the late Abdulkadir Ahmed. John Ebhodaghe was assisted by Dr. Wole Adewunmi and Abdullahi Mahmoud who were appointed Executive Directors and heads of the only two divisions created that was the Operations Division and Finance and Administration Division. The Managing Director also came along to his new beat with a formidable small team from the Central Bank to help him put the NDIC on a sound footing. Abdulkadir Ahmed, the Governor of CBN continued to closely supervise the fledgling corporation as Chairman of the NDIC Board of Directors.

Thus, when Umaru reported in May 1989, he found himself among a small group of not more than fifty Nigerians from diverse backgrounds to form the nucleus of the pioneer staff of the NDIC. Quite a number of this pioneer staff was from the CBN, some were from other banks, others like him were from the federal and state services, and many from other institutions spread around the country. Some of the pioneer staff Umaru met on arrival at the NDIC headquarters were late Dr. Rufa'i Umar Madaki, his classmate at Rumfa College, who later became Managing Director NEXIM, Mohammed Kabir Ahmed who later became Director General PENCOM, late Fatima Balaraba Ibrahim who later became a Minister of the Federal Republic of Nigeria, Barrister A. B. Nyako, Barrister G. O. Kembi, F. Ilen-Otuma, Mrs. Dan Nzelu, Mrs. C. E. Afabor, Muhammad Uthman, O. M. Suleiman, B. D. Umar, D. I. Isabu andNwaboze Orji. These and some others were the pioneer staff of NDIC that Umaru found on ground, ready to tend the young institution and help it grow.

Getting Started

Umaru was posted as the first Deputy Director to head the Financial and Technical Support Department. He was excited and looked forward to settling down into this fresh assignment, which was entirely new to him. The department was responsible for monitoring the health of all the Nigerian banks with a view to identifying their weaknesses and sorting out those that needed intervention so that they could be given financial support and temporary relief. But then as head of a new unit, he had to sit with his staff to work out the framework for the financial support to the banks.

According to Umaru, the early challenges had to do with establishing the organisation itself, getting the right organisational structure, the right framework, the right people and then creating awareness in establishing the right relationship with all the components such as the bankers, the Central Bank and the general public. The earliest challenge for management was to establish rules and regulations, internal policies, whether they are audit policies or HR policies, or purchases. The operational arm was very critical. They had to assemble the right people, give them the right training and had them ready to participate especially in the area of monitoring and examination of banks. This was only possible by establishing the kind of information they wanted to collect on monthly or quarterly basis to help undertake what is called 'offsite' examination of the banks.

As the NDIC was a new establishment, they had to design all those formats and returns. They also needed to know the kind of returns expected from the banks so as to know their operations and to know the risks NDIC was going to be carrying as an insurer. They also had to get the right IT platform to facilitate the operations. In due course, NDIC had to establish its own IT policy, programs, training and infrastructure so as to enable it discharge its responsibilities adequately and to interface with the banking system. That was quite a challenge for Umaru and his colleagues.

Thirdly, in the Financial and Technical Support Department, they had to come up with a policy that would guide them, with the approval of the Board, regarding how they assess the performance of the banks. They had to determine at what stage should a bank need support for instance, what condition should warrant that, how much support to give, at what price do they give it, and what would be the condition of granting it. They had to work out all this and let everybody know about it. The same goes for what is called technical support. NDIC had to establish that policy framework afresh.

As for bank examination, fortunately the CBN was already conducting that. And as many of the pioneer staff, including the pioneer Managing Director, came from the Central Bank it was not difficult for them to adopt the format and the framework of the bank examination. The task then was to train other staff, the fresh hands, to be able to go to the banks and examine them. So, all these were ab initio very challenging. Nevertheless, in due course when the banks started having serious liquidity problems as a result of the sudden withdrawal of government deposits and the escalation of foreign exchange, many of these theories Umaru and his colleagues learnt about bailout and so on had to come into play immediately.

While handling the challenges of setting up a new department, Umaru and his colleagues had to also wade through a tome of literature from the World Bank, the IMF, and the United States Federal Deposit Insurance Corporation (FDIC). The World Bank and the IMF had collaborated actively with the Central Bank to set up the NDIC, more or less, on the template of the FDIC of the United State. And to soak up the literature and gain further exposure, the staff members were also sent on various courses organised by the World Bank and the IMF. All the newly-recruited employees of the NDIC were sent to the Central Bank Training Centre for the foundation course as well as advanced courses in bank management and examination. All the programmes were examinable. Umaru participated in all these programmes along with all the newly recruited staff and they were required to pass all the examinations before the confirmation of their appointments. Performance in the examination also determined postings and future prospects in the NDIC. It was these kinds of transparent yardsticks that really formed the very good foundation for inculcating the right work etiquettes, culture and value system in the staff of NDIC.

    Umaru then settled down in his new department and quickly got used to its functions. Even though the bank failures were still one or two years ahead, it was the solid foundation that Umaru and his colleagues laid in the Financial and Technical Support Department that really prepared the NDIC to adequately handle the multiple bank failures that came up in the 1990s. Explaining the functions of the department more graphically Umaru said, "The department, like the name suggested, was like a rehabilitation centre, something like an intensive care unit (ICU) of a hospital where sick banks could be identified through effective monitoring, supervision and examination, so that they could be isolated, diagnosed and possibly rehabilitated, under our watchful eyes, as it were. Of course, if the rehabilitation fails, there is no more you can do to assist the patient."

Stormy Days in the Banking Sector

It was exciting working in a new agency and taking charge of a new department with a new schedule of duties. Umaru settled down to work immediately. Of course, there were teething problems with movement and settling down in Lagos, but he was fortunate that the NDIC had anticipated all these and had made adequate provisions to cushion the jolting effect. The corporation had made arrangements to house its executive staff in guest houses and hotels before accommodation could be procured or rented for them. Umaru, along with two other colleagues of his, Dr. Omar Rufa'i and Dr. Wole Adewunmi, were accommodated in a guest house in Victoria Island. The arrangement made it possible for them to compare notes, rub minds and learn from each other on a daily basis. In due course, he relocated his family from Kano.

Calm before the Storm

Meanwhile, in the larger society, mostly congregated around Lagos, then the political, financial and commercial capital of Nigeria, momentous decisions were being taken that would precipitate the young corporation which was just a few months old into action that would throw it right into the vortex of the national financial cauldron. It would be recalled that in July 1986, during the early days of the reign of General Ibrahim Babangida, the Federal Government had introduced the Structural Adjustment Programme (SAP). The introduction of the programme was as a result of the collapse of oil prices at the international market. In the 1980s, oil was the main revenue earner of the Nigerian economy in the mid-

1980s, as it is today. This necessitated the restructuring of the economy in order to address the sharp drop in oil revenue in the economy. One of the key areas targeted by SAP was the financial sector. The thrust of the programme in the financial sector was to deregulate and allow the emergence of new institutions and pave the way for the exit of the weak ones in the sector in order to address their irregularities in the financial market, particularly the banking sector.

The deregulation policy of the sector resulted into a precipitous upsurge in the number of banks, both merchant and commercial. As at 1987, there were 47 banks but the number rose sharply to 81 by 1989 and snowballed to 120 in 1990. On the one hand, the phenomenal increase in the number of banks had salutary effects on the financial services industry, as banking services became far more accessible to the generality of the populace. On the other hand, however, the liberalisation of the financial system also paved the way for some businessmen to set up banking institutions which they saw as avenues for making quick and easy money without any regard to the adverse effects on the performance of their banks and the general stability of the banking system. The deregulation of interest and exchange rates and the resultant persistent wide gap between the official and the so-called parallel market exchange rates made banking business most tempting and lucrative to these investors to enjoy phantom financial returns. That was why the banking industry quickly started showing signs of distress, even before NDIC was created. It was on record that one year before the creation of NDIC, seven banks were already declared to be technically insolvent.

That was the scenario in 1989 when the situation was further compounded by the Federal Government's decision towards the end of the year to move all public sector funds from commercial and merchant banks to the Central Bank of Nigeria (CBN). The decision, which took immediate effect, caused major liquidity crisis in the banking industry. Some of the banks could not honour their obligations to their depositors. Some were even finding it difficult to meet their obligations at the inter-bank market transactions. These developments obviously caused panic and created serious doubts and concern about the entire banking system.

The Eye of the Storm

The NDIC itself was then just a few months old. Umaru and his colleagues were just settling into their new roles when they found themselves thrown unexpectedly into the eye of the storm. The banks had started failing and exhibiting problems of under-capitalisation, persistent illiquidity, deterioration of assets quality, frauds and poor management. As more of them started to show more signs of stress, it became incumbent on the NDIC to swing into action to safeguard depositors' funds and the banks assets as well. Fortunately, part of the mandate of the NDIC was to provide financial and technical support to deserving insured institutions. The NDIC propelled into action immediately to assess the seriousness of the liquidity problems, one bank after the other. The CBN, also, as part of its prompt response, set up a Crisis Management Committee with the NDIC as an active participant. The report of that committee provided a basis for the intervention that took place, whereby the CBN and NDIC provided 'accommodation bills' to banks that were in dire need of liquidity support. The crisis affected many banks at the time and had to be shored up with public funds of about ₦2.3 billion. The intervention was not only financial but also technical by way of giving critical assistance to the affected banks.

In the words of Umaru, "that was what was called 'cease and desist order'. It is like your doctor telling you, 'Okay, take this tablet for the next two months, but don't do this, don't do that'. We had to reel out orders to them. Some of them, of course, ended up being taken over virtually by the CBN/NDIC because of their inability to manage their affairs in a way that would not endanger public funds. Some of the stringent requirements were the streamlining of branches to curtail unregulated expansion and curtail staff costs, rationalising operational costs and embarking on aggressive debt recovery. We were constantly monitoring these measures just like in the case of your bank giving you a loan to establish a business, such a bank will want to look at your books and monitor your actions. It will advise you to take steps that will ensure that your business is profitable so that you can repay your loan."

The 'cease and desist' orders were imposed on many banks to help stabilise their financial conditions. In due course, a sizeable proportion of them had to be temporarily taken over and managed by NDIC and the CBN. Eventually, those that were severely distressed were acquired, restructured and sold to new investors.

The intervention arrested the ugly situation and promptly doused the tension and panic among the populace, it also restored confidence in the banking system. Most of the beneficiary banks, with the exception of a few, repaid the loans in good time. Those that could not meet up with the obligations to pay their debts and whose conditions worsened progressively were subsequently liquidated. That was a big test for the young corporation within its short existence, and rising up to meet the challenge frontally was a major confidence boosting achievement for it. At least as at 1995, eighteen distressed banks were taken over by CBN/NDIC, more than half of them on their paths to liquidation.

It must have been quite a difficult action for the NDIC to liquidate a bank because it meant not only loss of both public and private funds, but also loss of jobs and livelihood for citizens. This was even more pronounced in a developing country like Nigeria where both funds and jobs were in short supply. However, the corporation had to do the needful at that critical period in order to save the entire banking system from the devastating effect of the distress syndrome.

At every event of a distressed bank, the CBN/NDIC was mandated to post its full time senior staff to take over and run the bank for a period of time until normalcy returned or the bank was wound up. In 1995, there were 18 of such distressed banks taken over by the NDIC/CBN. Umaru was sent to partner as an Executive Director in the three-member interim management board of the First African Trust Bank (FATB), whose fortunes were brought to its knees by the squabbles among its owners, leading to its being distressed and the eventual take over by CBN/NDIC. It was a great learning experience for him as it gave him a ground-level view of distress, its tragic consequences and actions to be taken by the regulatory authorities to solve the problem. His experience at FATB impacted him greatly and it bolstered his resolve to always take the necessary preventive measures to avoid distressed situation in banks, and whenever it unavoidably happened, to see that the matter was resolved with minimum hardship on both the depositors and staff of the bank.

Sojourn in the National Institute

At the turn of the millennium, Umaru was nominated as a participant on the one-year long course at the prestigious National Institute of Policy and Strategic Studies (NIPSS), Kuru. It is a highly sought annual nomination which is open to only the highest rung of the Federal and State Civil Service, the Armed Forces, the Police and other para-military organs, plus a sprinkling of high valued executives from the private sector organisations. The nomination to attend the course is cherished among public officers. This is because since it was established in 1979, the National Institute has continued to serve as a high level centre of research, dialogue and reflection for the high calibre citizens of the country. Obasanjo who established NIPSS during his military regime had said, "The idea for the Institute was inspired and informed by my experience at the Royal College of Defence Studies in London in 1974."

Umaru had sought for the nomination at this juncture of his career because he believed that he had garnered enough experience both from his Kano State Civil Service career and the over ten years he had then spent in NDIC would enable him to participate meaningfully among his peers at the National Institute. It also gave him a break to have some fresh air and an opportunity to return to the classroom to reflect on many issues. He recalled that even when he was a Permanent Secretary in Kano State, there were attempts to send him to Kuru but the pressure of work at that time did not allow him to go.

Umaru joined the Senior Executive Course 23 at Kuru in February 2001 and was to remain there till graduation in November 2001. He joined an elite group from all walks of life in the country; from the Police, SSS, the Military, Federal and State Civil Services, and captains of industries. Some of the members of Umaru' set include Engr. Mohammed Gambo Umar, Managing Director of Kapital Insurance, who served as Monitor-General, Brigadier (Dr.) Bernard Abang who later became Director Medical Services of the Nigerian Army, DIG Bello Labaran, Rear Admiral N.I. Dirisu, Engr. Baba Gana Zanna, then Director-General, National Directorate of Employment (NDE), Dr. Sani Sufi, a Director in the Federal Civil Service, Mohammed Ghali Umar who became Ambassador to Egypt and later Chief of Protocol to President Umaru Musa Yar'Adua, General (Dr.) James Ojukwu another Director Medical Services of the Nigerian Army, Lai Lasunde who became Ambassador to Angola, Nwakanma Umelo who became Ambassador to Belgium and several others.

The Institute is located in a beautiful environment by a lake in Kuru which is very close to Vom. General Garba made the National Institute even more beautiful by adopting a kind of horticulture that transformed the campus into one of the prettiest in the country. He even developed a golf course within the grounds of the campus. The stay in Kuru was fully residential and as the National Institute does not have a teaching faculty as in a university, the one-year course was largely run on a system of self-study based on lectures delivered by invited prominent and distinguished personalities. The experience and expertise of these guest lecturers, drawn from all sectors of national life, are tapped to stimulate the thinking of participants.

That particular year, 2001, the course was inaugurated by the Secretary of the Government of the Federation (SGF) and throughout the length of the course they were variously lectured by Federal Government ministers, top officers of the armed forces, distinguished ambassadors, scholars and leading politicians. Seminars were held within discussions groups under the guidance of the Director of Studies and his moderators to critically discuss every lecture delivered to derive lessons. Also, towards the end of the course, the participants were required to write a long essay on a subject matter that showcased their expertise and experience.

National, African and European Tours

During the course, three tours were undertaken, namely, a local tour, which involved visits by group of participants to various states within Nigeria, a tour of selected African countries, and a tour of selected countries outside Africa. For the national tour, Umaru's group went to Jigawa State where they spent a week assessing the social and economic conditions of the state with a focus on ecological issues such as desertification, issues of drought, challenges to agriculture, challenges to ecology and how they all affect livelihood and economic conditions of the people. They toured all the major towns such as Hadejia, Gumel, Kazaure, Birnin Kudu, and Dutse the capital where they rounded up with a session with the Governor, Saminu Turaki.

The African and world tours were undertaken later in the year. Before embarking on the tours, the groups were always extensively briefed on each country to be visited, first, by the staff of the Studies Department in NIPSS and then also by the staff of the Ministry of Foreign Affairs which in any case would be involved in arranging the tours. On arrival, the host government and functionaries would take over and guide the groups and also provide briefings throughout the visit. At the conclusion of each visit, the groups would each produce a report based on their findings.

The first trip outside Nigeria was for the African tour. Umaru's group undertook a memorable trip to Namibia. It was a very interesting tour for the group because Namibia, a young independent nation, was just coming out of the apartheid era with all the usual problems of lack of educational facilities and indigenous manpower to run the country. In the course of going around the country, the study group found many Nigerians serving in various capacities in their hospitals, schools, and even in the judiciary. The study group was led by the Director-General of NIPSS, late General Joseph Garba, a colourful Nigerian Foreign Minister in the 1970s, during whose tenure Namibian leaders, then fighting a liberation war, received a lot of attention from Nigeria including solid financial support. Thus, due more to the presence of the General leading the group, they were accorded a royal treatment throughout the visit.

Apart from the African tour, they also did a world tour which involved visiting a number of countries in different parts of the world. Umaru's group went to Europe to visit France for a study tour that lasted over a week. The intention was to get an insight into the policy of the French Government towards Africa, particularly Nigeria. Their visit covered the Foreign Ministry, the International Institute of Foreign Affairs and the military high command for Africa where they received useful briefings.

The Long Essay

As a partial fulfilment of the requirement for the award of Membership of the National Institute (mni), Umaru undertook a long essay on a subject truly close to his heart: the Control and Management of Distressed Banks in Nigeria. The study which approached the issue of distress from a micro angle used the example of the events that culminated in the collapse of the First African Trust Bank (FATB) in the early 1990s. Umaru watched the resultant actions taken by the regulatory authorities to resolve the problem at close range because he was part of the team sent from NDIC to superintend the affairs of FATB before it was finally sold to a group of investors. The essay was so informative that NIPSS in later years allowed its publication as a book to serve as a reference point to Nigerian policy makers and scholars in the quest for remedies against distress in the banking industry.

NIPSS a Worthwhile Experience

Umaru described his stay at the National Institute as a worthwhile experience. He spoke at length about the participants, the facilitators, the guest lecturers and the group study. He said, "We had participants from various professions, various disciplines, from the military, police, and other security services, diplomats and representatives of chambers of commerce and manufacturers. It was a highly diversified group of participants who brought a lot of knowledge and experience to all the discussions and assignments we had. The classes were manageable in number, not more than four study groups, comprising ten to eleven persons in each group. We were lucky to have facilitators from the military and academia. That was in addition to the guest lecturers who could be ministers, ambassadors, subject-matter experts on anything on the table, whether one is talking about global warming, conflicts, agriculture or the environment. And we had interesting interactive sessions with them."

He also gave a glowing testimony to the Director-General of that time General Joseph Garba. The General was one of the key military officers in the Murtala/Obasanjo regime (1975-79) where he held the post of Foreign Minister. Later in the 1980s, he became Nigeria's Ambassador and Permanent Representative to the United Nations and went on to crown it by becoming the President of the 44th United Nations General Assembly from 19th September 1989 to 17th September 1990. At the conclusion of his assignment, he became a Senior Research Fellow under the auspices of the Carnegie Corporation and the Ford Foundation before the new civilian administration invited him to become Director-General of the National Institute.

Umaru said, "And then we were very lucky to have the late General Joe Garba as Director-General who was very serious, hardworking, professional, and an upright nationalist who had a passion for excellence. Under his leadership, we were really grilled in Kuru, not only academically but also socially. It wasn't just about academics but about building a team with a crop of individuals, coming from different walks of life. He was extremely passionate not only about NIPSS but also about our set. We cultivated a very close relationship with him such that he knew all of us, every one of us, by our first names. He would invite us to his house in Jos and also to his country home in Langtang to host us. He cultivated close relationship with every one of us taking time to know the potential of each one of us. He was extremely supportive and was always there for us unless he was not in town".

General Garba was said to place a lot of premium on the social interpersonal networking that could be established among participants in that unique setting. He believed that there couldn't have been a better opportunity to create that kind of serious empathy between potential leaders in the country so that the participants after the course in NIPSS would continue to relate with one another at all times.

General Garba was a very charismatic leader who helped to keep the participants focussed on their assignment. Umaru said, "You feel his presence always. He would always be there during our lunch hours. So long as he is in town you would start the lunch with him, you would finish with him and nobody left the cafeteria until he left. So that even during lunch he would have time with you to sit and chat on issues. And on weekly basis he would make sure that each participant had a one-to-one, to discuss any topic, with him. That way he too learnt from you. But we learnt a lot from him, about his role in the military, his days as a young Foreign Minister, his role in the liberation struggle for the independence of Namibia, Angola, Zimbabwe and South Africa, how Nigeria got its rightful place as a frontline state in the liberation of those states under Apartheid domination, his encounter with General Murtala Mohammed and General Olusegun Obasanjo. His leadership was always about patriotism, love for one another, understanding our diversity and the need to engage one another, understand each other so that we could collectively help address our national problem as a developing country. It is a pity we lost him at his prime".

At the conclusion of the course, Umaru left Kuru very much fulfilled. He returned to NDIC to take charge of the Corporate Development Department which at the time was in charge of strategic planning and change management within the organisation.

NDIC – The Millennium Years

In early 2001, Umaru returned to his duty post after attending a course at the National Institute in Jos. He was far more informed, adequately prepared and well-motivated to face the challenges of high office as a direct benefit from his participation in the course. He was warmly received by his staff in the Corporate Development Department where he departed to attend a course at the National Institute. While he was away, a new Managing Director, Mr. Ganiyu Ogunleye, was appointed to replace Mr. John Ebhodaghe, the pioneer Managing Director who had completed his tenure after two terms in office.

By the time Umaru resumed duties, the new Managing Director had already settled in office. However, Umaru was already familiar with Mr. Ganiyu Ogunleye just like the rest of the management staff as he was not a stranger to NDIC. He had joined the Central Bank immediately after graduation and had spent a greater part of twenty-five years of his working life in the Banking Supervision Department where he was closely associated (along with the first Managing Director, John Ebhogade) with the NDIC from its embryonic stage. At a later stage, he had also represented the CBN on the Management Committee of NDIC after the dissolution of the Board in 1996 till 1999. The Management Committee played the role of the Board pending the reconstitution of a new

Board of Directors. Therefore, besides his contributions at the planning stages of the NDIC, he also served on the Board of the Corporation before being elevated to the post of Managing Director.

Mr. Ganiyu Ogunleye Adewale led the management team, which included Umaru at the helm of affairs in the Corporate Affairs Department, for ten years. The millennium years were an exciting period for all government institutions in Nigeria as they coincided with the return to civilian rule which offered fresh hope for the country and the conduct of its affairs in a more open and democratic manner.

According to the former Managing Director, on assumption of office, he worked closely with his fellow Directors and other staff and emphasised on issues pertaining to Banking Supervision and Failure Resolution. His desire was to professionalise the workforce and create a credible and efficient organisation. Towards the proper positioning of the corporation, the vision and mission statements as well as its core values were developed and codified. The corporation also deployed adequate resources to capacity building with emphasis on training and development so as to upgrade its human resources.

The management also reviewed the organogram it inherited and created new departments and units to facilitate efficient service delivery. Some departments such as the Receivership and Liquidation Department was split into two namely; Asset Management and Claims Resolution Departments. The Enterprise Risk Management Unit, the Performance Management Unit and the Special Insured Institutions Departments were also created.

A new deposit insurance legislation was enacted in 2006 to take care of the perceived problems that were encountered from inception. As part of the new legislation, there was an upward review of the insurance coverage per depositor, from ₦50000 to ₦200000. The legislation also extended the deposit insurance coverage of ₦100000 per depositor to Microfinance Banks and Primary Mortgage Banks with effect from January 2008. Apart from these limits set by the law, protection by the scheme could be expanded beyond the basic insurance limit by the payment of uninsured deposits through liquidation dividends.

NDIC's Supervisory Role

During this period, NDIC turned its attention fully to the reassessment of its supervisory role so as to ensure that banking operations would continue to be conducted in a safe and sound manner and in compliance with laid down rules, laws and regulations. It jettisoned the Rule and Compliance-Based System of supervision and adopted the Risk-Based System acclaimed to be a more proactive supervisory process which focused attention on the risk profile of the supervised financial institutions. The Risk-Based Supervision enables the bank supervisor to develop a supervisory package for each bank, and proactively monitor and supervise banks to facilitate the attainment of the objective of the promotion of soundness, safety and stability of the financial system.

Despite having a good supervisory system over the banks, failures sometimes occur. That is why one of the major policy objectives of putting in place a Deposit Insurance System (DIS) is to provide an orderly mechanism for failure resolution. Since inception, the

NDIC in collaboration with the CBN had allowed the use of traditional market-based solution to strengthen the operations of a bank that was showing signs of failure. Such measures included injection of fresh capital to reinvigorate the failing bank, a merger with, or acquisition by, a healthy bank among others. These efforts did not impose a cost on NDIC. Whenever banks failed, the licensing authority would have to take decisive action of withdrawing their operating licenses. For example, in 1994 and 1995 when it was realised that all possible means of resolving the distressed condition of some banks have been exhausted, the CBN/NDIC decided to invoke the provisions of Banks and Financial Institutions (BOFI), Act No. 25 of 1991, to revoke the operating licenses of five banks, with the approval of the Head of State. The affected banks were Kapital Merchant Bank, Financial Merchant Bank, Alpha Merchant Bank, United Merchant Bank, Republic Bank and more banks failed in the following years, such that by 1998 the number of failed banks had gone up to 31.

Purchase and Assumption (P&A)

Thus, at the turn of the millennium, a new approach to bank resolution was becoming popular. It was the Purchase and Assumption (P&A) failure resolution mechanism. In these circumstances, a healthy bank is allowed to purchase some or all the assets and liabilities of a failed bank through negotiations. This kind of transaction ensures the protection of all depositors, thereby giving credibility to the deposit insurance scheme. It also ensures continuity of banking services, thereby engendering confidence in the banking system and also helps to promote market discipline as shareholders of the failed bank might not be paid. It is obviously less disruptive to the economy than many of the failure resolution options. It is in this manner that Trade Bank, Eagle Bank, Hallmark Bank, among others were successfully taken over by healthy banks with minimum disruption during Ganiyu Ogunleye's tenure. The banks were duly recapitalised by the new investors and business continued as usual.

Challenges

As in every human endeavour, the NDIC faced various challenges in the pursuit of its mandate of deposit guarantee, banking supervision, failure resolution and liquidation. With regards to deposit guarantee, they realised that despite the existence of NDIC for over ten years, the concept itself was not properly understood. Generally, people confuse deposit insurance which is a safety-net facility with conventional insurance which is a commercial contract. Many others perceive NDIC's liquidation role as equivalent to being an undertaker rather than being a deposit protector which is what it is. Even though this wrong perception is not peculiar to Nigeria, NDIC made strenuous efforts to educate stakeholders through seminars and workshops held in various parts of the country.

With respect to supervision, the challenges NDIC encountered relate to the unreliability of returns rendered by banks, particularly because they wanted to minimise the premium liability which was routinely paid to NDIC. However, such attempts were contained through premium examination by very efficient and highly trained NDIC examiners. As attested by Lamido Sanusi Lamido, the Governor of the CBN during that period, the banks usually shivered whenever they were to be examined by the NDIC examiners.

The greatest challenge the NDIC encountered during the period was related to failure resolution. Under the military regime where decrees were in force and the Failed Bank Tribunals were established, failure resolution was easier to implement. But in the democratic dispensation, the decrees were abrogated and issues of failure resolution had to go through the normal courts processes with all the effects and consequences of delays and other attendant problems. To worsen matters, bank owners with strong political connections attempted to use either the courts or political leverage to reverse the revocation of their banking licenses. There was the classic case of Savannah Bank whose promoter, Jim Nwobodo, was a serving Senator at the time the bank was to be liquidated. The NDIC Managing Director and the CBN Governor, Dr. Joseph Sanusi, were put under serious pressure to prevent the liquidation of the bank. Senator Jim Nwobodo even dragged them before both the Senate and House of Representatives to justify the basis for the revocation of Savannah Bank's license.

In addition to the foregoing, politically-exposed persons who were indebted to failed banks sought unmerited interest waivers. Some sought the intervention of the supervising ministers but fortunately none of the ministers intervened. Others resorted to blackmail in an attempt to evade fulfilling their debt obligations. But such antics did not sway the position of the NDIC management. They refused to be intimidated.

Another big challenge to failure resolutions was the position of state-owned banks. When such banks were found to be insolvent and terminally distressed, the owners, who were either unwilling or unable to recapitalise their banks, resisted the revocation of their licenses and liquidation of such banks. Bank of the North, owned by the northern states, was a good example. Given its political underpinnings and the resistance put up by the owners, the NDIC management had to seek audience with President Obasanjo in September 2004 to request for his intervention. The President was able to put pressure on the prominent bad debtors to pay up. The management also met the northern state governors twice to discuss the bank's problems. All these efforts fortunately paid off eventually when over ₦10 billion was recovered due to the intervention of the President and the Governors.

Movement within the Corporation

When Umaru came to NDIC, he was posted to the Financial and Technical Department as its pioneer head. Within a short period of one year, the department pioneered the establishment of a framework for the identification and management of problem-prone banks. That was the framework that made it possible for the corporation to start rendering technical support to insured institutions whenever the need arose. The assistance that amounted to over ₦1 billion at that time was handled in conjunction with the CBN. The benefitting institutions were expected to pay back the loan within a period of 1 to 2 years. Most of them paid back but a few could not, due to reasons that included huge non-performing loans, poor and weak credit policy, poor corporate governance and unwholesome insider dealings. Others suffered due to macro-economic challenges such as the currency devaluation and poor commodity prices.

Umaru would later be posted to the Personnel Department as a full Director where he was to operate for many years. It was, for him, the beginning of a functional shift from the operational to the human resources section within the corporation. He was a perfect fit for the department considering his pedigree as a former Kano State Permanent Secretary and also a former Secretary, Water Resources Engineering and Construction Company (WRECA) in Kano, where he was directly involved in human resources management.

The issues were challenging all the same, as NDIC a new organisation had to come up with new policies and fresh approaches to deal with all sorts of capacity building and staff matters. They had to come up with personnel recruitment, manpower development, disciplinary policies and a variety of other issues affecting staff welfare. The department had to come up with a policy framework to guide the young corporation. Umaru compared his role as the Head of Department to that of a bridge as he performed some kind of bridge-making functions between the management and employees. Staff would always want more and more from the management and directors would have to be the bridge, more or less. It was not an easy job at all as both sides would have demands and expectations that have to be properly managed and met. The challenge then was to integrate staff development and motivation with the expectations of higher performance. It is on record that Umaru performed his role as a mediator excellently well. The department was able to get NDIC to partner with relevant international organisations such as the World Bank, International Monetary Fund (IMF), International Association for Deposit Insurers, Federal Deposit Insurance Corporation to benefit from their knowledge, especially in the areas of bank supervision and liquidation.

Umaru was later moved to head the Administration Department. One of the most important tasks he performed was to pioneer the acquisition of lands in Abuja for the building of a new Head Office. Even though Abuja had been named the Federal Capital in 1976, it was only in 1991 that the President moved his office and residence there and followed it up with a pronouncement that all Federal Government offices domiciled in Lagos should prepare to follow suit. For the NDIC, that meant looking for suitable plot of land in Abuja to erect a befitting office and also look into the possibility of finding decent accommodation for the staff. The assignment was handed down to the Administration Department and Umaru spearheaded the look-out for a plot of land for building the new Head Office as well as initiating the due process for the engagement of a suitable contractor to start work on the project. NDIC generously got enough land to build the head office as well as land for other structures around Maitama, Asokoro, Karimo and Wuse districts. He also initiated the discussion with the Federal Housing Authority (FHA) for the acquisition of housing units to provide decent accommodation for NDIC staff who were moving to Abuja.

By 1997 when a firm directive was issued by the Federal Government to all its agencies and departments that were still in Lagos to move to Abuja, the NDIC was one of the few agencies which were in a comfortable position to comply with the directive. They had a few logistic problems as the building was not fully ready. Umaru recalled that Abuja was still empty. The Head Office was not fully ready, nevertheless they had to move.

At least the lights were working, there was water and the lifts were functioning. But most of the jobs were not finished. Offices were not completed, neither partitioned nor allocated. The corporation had no option but to move and within a few months everything was sorted out.

The staff had a fairly easy time settling their families in Abuja. NDIC was one of the few government agencies to have acquired some seventy to eighty units of houses from FHA for its staff – the two-bedroom apartment houses for as little as ₦350,000. The corporation did not only acquire the houses but also renovated, fenced and provided all the facilities for the staff to have a decent living quarters in Abuja. In fact, the movement to Abuja was so successful that NDIC hardly needed to rent any property in Abuja when they moved in. All the NDIC members of staff were accommodated. Those who opted out of the arrangement and needed to take housing allowance were allowed to do so.

Preparation for Retirement

As the millennium years gain speed, Umaru started to prepare for retirement. He is someone that knew the value of preparation for retirement as he had spent a good portion of the time in NDIC preparing staff for retirement. He began his public service career in 1975 and would have clocked 35 years by 2010. In 2007 he had psyched himself to retirement shortly and had even packed from NDIC official quarters to his personal house. As God would will it, the Executive Director in charge of Finance and Administration, Fatima Balaraba Ibrahim, was named a Minister by President Umaru Musa Yar'Adua. That created a vacuum which Umaru was elevated to fill. He thus crossed over from Management to join the Board of Directors as an Executive Director, Corporate Services.

As Executive Director, he provided leadership at a wider and more strategic level. In his words, "I ensured proper alignment and integration among all departments under the division (i.e. Information Technology, Human Resource, Administration and Finance Departments) with a view to ensuring that our systems and processes were continuously fine-tuned for efficiency and enhancement of staff capabilities and development. I ensured proper interface with other external stakeholders, for example, National Assembly, Central Bank of Nigeria, Federal Ministry of Finance and others. I played a key role as a member of the Executive Committee and Board of NDIC."

At The Helm of Affairs

Towards the end of 2009, both the Managing Director Ganiyu Ogunleye and the Executive Director (Operations), Prof Peter Umoh, retired after two terms in office. Umaru was appointed acting Managing Director. In his words, "I was left alone under the able support and guidance of the Board of Directors. Internally I ensured that the management team was carried along in all major decisions so as to ensure cohesion and collaboration, good governance and shared responsibilities. I enjoyed good relationship with the Board which translated into the initiation of good policies and programmes. I was supported by the Federal Ministry of Finance, had good relationship with the National Assembly and collaborated well with the Central Bank of Nigeria and Bankers' Committee to ensure that the corporation added value to the banking system."

Managing Director

After about a year, Umaru was finally confirmed as Managing Director/Chief Executive of the corporation. It was a trying moment for the banking industry in Nigeria just recuperating from the financial meltdown of 2008/9. It required the right leadership at the level of supervisory institutions such as the NDIC to steer the banks from the dangers of the cliffs.

NDIC under Umaru Ibrahim

With Alhaji Umaru Ibrahim at the helm of affairs at the NDIC, the Board and Management have achieved a lot of positives and taken tremendous strides to further enhance public confidence in the banking sector in Nigeria.

The NDIC, between 2009 and 2013, effected an upward review of deposit insurance coverage level to boost the confidence of the public in the financial system. Previously, the maximum deposit insurance coverage levels were ₦200,000 and ₦100,000 for Deposit Money Banks, Micro Finance Banks/Primary Mortgage Banks, respectively. However, it was increased to ₦500,000 and ₦200,000 for Deposit Money Banks and MFBs and PMBS respectively. Furthermore, the coverage level for PMBs was further reviewed up to ₦500,000 in 2015. In further display of visionary leadership, deposit insurance coverage was also extended to non-interest Islamic Banks as well as subscribers of mobile money operations all in an effort to bring financial services closer to people.

The management of NDIC also developed a board charter and instituted better corporate governance practices. The Board approved the development of appropriate job roles, responsibilities and key performance indicators for the Board, Board Committees and Senior Management to assist in the discharge of their respective functions. That initiative also formed the basis with which the activities and performance of the Board, Board Committees and Management could be appraised.

As previously highlighted, the operation of a deposit insurance scheme is not without its challenges, and unfortunately when these challenges crystallize, the depositors are the ones who suffer the consequences. The case of Savannah bank is a perfect example of where the NDIC Act No. 16 of 2006 failed in protecting the depositors. As a result, as MD, Umaru Ibrahim sought to have the NDIC Act repealed and re-enacted to prevent a case like Savannah bank ever reoccurring. While the proposed amendment was passed by the House of Representatives of the 7th Assembly in 2015, the 7th assembly was dissolved before the Senate could pass the bill. This setback did not dissuade the MD as the proposed amendment is currently being reviewed by the 9th Assembly in 2020.

Risk-Based Auditing was also introduced to guide the corporation's internal control and risk reporting systems in line with best practices. The Board and Management, under Umaru Ibrahim, continues to support the implementation of Risk-Based Auditing (RBA) by providing the required resources needed for training and acquisition of software to be deployed for effective RBA.

For the first time in the over 20 years of the corporation, the Board Secretariat became formally a unit of the Legal Department, to specifically handle Board and Management matters.

Additional zonal offices were also established in order to enhance the operational capacity and ability of NDIC to meet its statutory mandate across the geo-political zones in the country. These offices are located in Port Harcourt, Yola and Sokoto.

The corporation also embarked on major capital projects. Some of these are the Lagos Office at Ikoyi, the Training Centre at Lekki, Lagos and the Head Office Annex at Abuja. The projects were in addition to the construction of Zonal Office buildings at Sokoto, Yola, Port Harcourt and Bauchi. The projects have commenced and it is expected that the completion of these projects will enhance NDIC's service delivery.

Information Technology drives the banking industry and financial sector. An assessment was conducted between 2008 and 2009 to review the ICT level of exposure and protection of the NDIC. As a result of the survey, the management of the corporation, under Umaru Ibrahim, conceptualised the ITSSA&A project in 2009. This project made it possible for a revamp of the NDIC's ICT system and infrastructure to conform with modern realities. The deployment officially commenced on 15th July, 2013. It provided a template for the continuous strengthening and enhancement of the NDIC's ICT infrastructure, going forward. In August 2013, the NDIC procured Automated Budget Management software to drive budget process and monitoring for effective Performance-Based Budget System.

The NDIC, under the watch of Umaru Ibrahim, also introduced Bridge Banking approach as a failure resolution option. That was not only innovative, it was also a novel approach to finding alternative ways to resolve bank failure rather than outright liquidation which usually had unpleasant consequences for stakeholders of the affected banks and also erode public confidence in the banking system. This neoteric approach birthed four bridge banks namely MainStreet Bank Ltd, Keystone Bank Ltd, Enterprise Bank Ltd and Polaris Bank Ltd. The Bridge Bank contrivance had a restorative effect on the banking system as it preserved and sustained operations of the four banks in all their branches and allowed over 3.7 million depositors to continue enjoying banking services in the premises of the affected banks. Jobs were also saved. The four affected banks at that time were Afribank PLC, Bank PHB PLC, Spring Bank PLC and Skye Bank PLC.

Regulatory agencies monitor operators of financial services' performance and their health, or lack thereof, through the returns they render at different frequencies. Banks and operators of financial services under the purview of the NDIC are required to submit their reports to the corporation. In order to aid ease of report generation, the process that was hitherto manual was automated through a software called electronic Financial Analyses and Surveillance System (e-FASS) jointly developed by CBN and NDIC. Another software developed by NDIC to ease liquidation process was the electronic Financial Institution Liquidation Management (e-FILMS). The e-FILMS web-system ensures access from all locations in NDIC, and potent functionality. That initiative has gone a long way in facilitating the work of the NDIC.

The NDIC, under its very modernistic CEO, places very high premium on staff training and human capital development. In view of this, the NDIC Academy was established and commissioned in May 2013. It is imperative to note that staff members of the corporation have undergone many specialised training programmes with world-class consultants and facilitators within and outside the country.

Another innovative approach to training and manpower development introduced by the Umaru administration in NDIC was to key into the Chartered Banker Masters in Business Administration (CB/MBA) developed by Bangor University, a leading Business Schools in Europe to enable staff to acquire relevant professional certificates. After a rigorous selection process in 2013, the corporation approved the sponsorship and enrolment of the first batch of twenty members of staff within the category of Management Assistant – Assistant Manager, not above the age of forty and had shown consistent track record of high performance in their assigned jobs. By 2016, a total of 77 staff were in enrolment spread across three batches and 68 have so far graduated from the programme, with two staff standing out exceptionally with distinction. In order to reduce cost, the programme has been designed to be mainly online, with a one-week residency visit to the University, and opportunity for a local examination centre at Bankers House in Lagos anchored by CIBN. The second stage of the programme continued in 2018.

In order to maintain a performance-driven culture in the work place, in line with the strategic vision of the NDIC, a seven-member committee was set up. Umaru Ibrahim mandated the committee to study and review the corporation's existing staff conditions of service vis-à-vis similar federal government agencies. It will be recalled that the conditions of service were last reviewed in 2006. The implementation of the committee's report as further boosted the productivity of the corporation's employees.

The business and operational environment of the financial industry is always evolving. This dynamism tends to leave regulators in a state of flux and it is sometimes a struggle for workers to effectively carry out statutory functions without compromising. Taking this into consideration, the Umaru Ibrahim-led NDIC proactively effected a review of the corporation's Code of Conduct handbook to a new and enhanced Culture handbook. That initiative was a masterstroke as it effectively provided an easy reference for NDIC staff and bank examiners as they carry out the onerous task of financial sector regulation in a fast-paced environment.

The NDIC installed IP-CCTV cameras in all its operating locations, especially at the Head Office building and zonal offices. That was in response to the security challenges experienced in the country. It was the desire of the CEO and management to create, not just a conducive atmosphere for its employees, but also to engender measures that would ensure the security of life and property within NDIC premises. Also worthy of note is the replacement of outdated elevators at the Head Office, and installation of modern firefighting devices.

Coping with the management of office space is a major challenge for many corporations. As business operations expand, so also will the need for more operating and functional work space arise. In combating this challenge, Umaru Ibrahim and his team introduced the Electronic Documents Management System (EDMS). The project, which entailed the electronic scanning and storage of documents, minimises storage space for documents and created a near-paperless office system. It also facilitates the ease of document retrieval and confidentiality of documents.

In order to drive operational efficiency, a Multimedia Digital Archiving System (MDAS) was introduced by Umaru Ibrahim and his management team. The MDAS software helped the NDIC in the effective pursuit of its public enlightenment programmes.

Umaru Ibrahim and his management team are always striving to entrench complete public confidence in the financial system through regulatory efforts aimed at ensuring a stable financial order. In the light of this, the foundation for extending financial assistance to worthy DMBs developed. The framework has two parts which are liquidity support and financial/ technical assistance.

In furtherance of the objective of establishing a stable financial order, the NDIC, under Umaru Ibrahim, strengthened the 'On-site Examination' of insured institutions in the system. The aim is to nip in the bud any adverse development in the institutions with a view to ensuring prompt corrective action through supervisory intervention. The corporation legally conducts routine examination of banks at least once every year. The NDIC also engages in special examination or investigation of banks. This happens when banks have been operating in a manner detrimental to its stakeholders or where a petition is received concerning the activities of the bank.

The Umaru Ibrahim-led management team introduced the assemblage of data into electronic platform. This project provides up-to-date information to stakeholders in the financial services sector, particularly sister regulatory agencies. In an unprecedented initiative, the management approved the development of an electronic database on debtors of failed banks.

In recognition of the power of the mass media, the NDIC involved them in its debt recovery efforts. That happened especially at the height of the failed banks' situation in Nigeria and recapitalisation of DMBs. The corporation, under Umaru Ibrahim, continuously engages in media broadcast of its activities and programmes for effective dissemination of information on its activities. This way, the public and all concerned stakeholders are kept abreast of the corporation's activities and developments at every point in time.

The public awareness campaign of the NDIC did not stop at mass media, but also extended to social media. The MD realised that an effective approach of engaging more youths in financial education was through social media platforms. As a result, the corporation in 2013 rolled out social media handles on Facebook, Twitter, Instagram, LinkedIn and Youtube. This strategy has been highly effective with thousands of followers on the different social media handles.

The generous spirit of Umaru Ibrahim is something all who know him can attest to. This spirit has permeated the culture of the corporation. Knowing that the NDIC has a social and moral obligation to aid in areas beyond the banking sector, Umaru Ibrahim has committed resources to ensure that the corporation plays its part in uplifting society. Under his astute leadership, the corporation has introduced a deposit insurance curriculum in 9 Nigerian universities, built academic blocks for several universities and secondary schools across the country, erected orphanages in less privileged local government and constructed bore holes for villages that do not have access to pipe-borne water.

When Umaru Ibrahim assumed office as the Chief Executive Officer of the NDIC, one of the problems he observed was that the staff strength of the corporation was heavy at the top and very lightweight at the bottom. He therefore initiated the recruitment of over 500 new staff. Prominence was given to the recruitment of the lower cadre of Management Assistants. The absence of that threatened succession planning in the corporation hitherto.

The NDIC management, under the leadership of Umaru Ibrahim, observed that the operators of Microfinance Banks lacked adequate knowledge to operate as practised in other climes. Many were not doing business as required and the objective of their existence was not being met. That development prompted the NDIC and other stakeholders (CBN, CIBN and FITC) to introduce an educational programme geared towards upscaling the knowledge of the operators and regulators in Microfinance banking.

According to Umaru, they were very lucky from day one in the NDIC because the founding fathers thought it wise to establish a wholesale comprehensive deposit insurance organisation that was tagged a 'Risk Minimiser'. This meant that the NDIC was not merely an agent of the CBN or a pay box whereby the CBN would close a bank, withdraw its license due to one reason or another and, because it was too busy, pass on the responsibility of settling the depositors of the closed bank to that institution. There were many deposit insurance organisations in the world, especially in Africa, that were fashioned along those lines that had no mandate to go into a bank to supervise, regulate or issue any form of sanctions to the bank. These organisations were just like collecting or paying agents to their Central Banks. Umaru opined that the NDIC was different.

As a specialised organisation, Umaru spoke more about the depth of the NDIC's powers. He said, "You cannot police or superintend any entity if you do not have sufficient laws behind you or sufficient independence. That is what makes us different from some institutions that have limited powers and mandates, operating more or less like glorified departments of their Central Banks."

He continued, "As far as the NDIC is concerned, we have the powers, just like the CBN, to supervise an insured bank. By law, when the CBN gives licence to a bank, we are almost automatically expected to insure the bank. The bank cannot refuse to be insured by us. It is automatic." He said that even though the NDIC would have preferred a situation whereby it was part of the process of licensing any new bank before insuring it, as the current system was burdensome, they could however live with the status quo for now in as much as the NDIC was operationally independent.

Talking more about the independence of the NDIC, Umaru said that the corporation had the power to examine any bank, to issue its report, to compel Boards and Managements to observe whatever advice that was given and to take steps to sanction them. He said, "We do these independently of the CBN, the Minister of Finance or anybody for that matter. As far as I know, I do not remember any matter that affected any insured bank wherein we took a position and somebody told us to go and change that position because the President or Vice President, Minister or Governor of the CBN didn't like it. However, that is not to say that if we take a position on your bank either as a customer, a director or a shareholder, you had no right to petition, complain or go to court. We are answerable, but nobody will wake up one morning and tell us not to do so and so like it happens in some cases in Nigeria."

Working in close collaboration with the CBN, having the right leadership, knowing the value of work, having the required level of independence and having the right motivation and skill – these are the different factors that has helped the NDIC weather the storms in the banking sector. Umaru said that right from 1994 when the NDIC started addressing the problems in the banking sector, it had to date placed in liquidation a total of 48 banks. In those days, when there were over a hundred banks in Nigeria, the NDIC deployed what was called 'Multiple Liquidation of Banks.' According to him, this meant that the NDIC could simultaneously liquidate five to six banks as the case may be. The rate of bank distress was highest during the military era right up to the General Abdulsalami Abubakar regime, after Sani Abacha, before civilian rule in 1999. In all of those times, the NDIC always enjoyed a high level of independence and non-interference from the powers that be. Umaru said he could not remember any time whereby the military government called to question their decisions as an agency.

Regarding the leadership of the NDIC then, the corporation was also favoured to be led by a very strong character in the person of late Mr. John Ebhodaghe, who enjoyed the backing of the Board, headed by former CBN governor, the late Alhaji Abdulkadir Ahmed who was highly respected. Everybody worked harmoniously to sanitise the banking industry during the period of deregulation and liberalisation of the economy. According to Umaru, the whole essence of establishing the NDIC was to assist in strengthening the system, by ensuring that the ailing banks, sick beyond redemption, were eased off the system in an orderly and professional manner.

The performance of any financial system is a function of the economy and there exists a symbiotic close relationship. The financial system is the engine of growth for the economy. Banks occupy a very strategic position in the economy by providing financial intermediate services and if a country's banks are sick, the effect on the economy can best be imagined.

According to Umaru, "We have come a long way after we experienced global financial crises from 2008 to 2010. We eventually came out of it and there were a lot of lessons that were learnt." He said factors that contributed to the problems of the banks had to do with issues like the quality of their boards and management, poor corporate governance and risk management, recklessness in terms of lending and so on. There were cases of gross insider abuses whereby privileged directors and shareholders helped themselves, their companies and cronies with large sums of credit, some of which were never meant to be repaid. Of course, there were other external factors such as the collapse of commodity prices, concentration of loans in the oil and gas sector, margin lending, etc.

Commenting on the situation today, Umaru described the banking system as 'largely stable' even though there were still some challenges. According to him, "There are banks that need to recapitalise. They need more funds, unfortunately, because of the growing deterioration of their assets." He also said that there were many bad loans in the sector that had reached the 15 per cent mark or more. He admitted that this was quite high because typically, the level of loan delinquency allowed for any bank was about five per cent. He attributed the reasons for this to be both domestic and external.

Further to the above, Umaru enjoined the banks to show more seriousness in tackling the issue of non-performing loans in their books. He advised them saying, "To the banks themselves, one would like to see a situation whereby the loans are settled to fill up the vacuums created in the first place." He opined that this would go a long way in opening up new credit opportunities for other borrowers in critical sectors like manufacturing, agriculture, service, real estate, etc. This would in turn lead to improvement in the economy.

Visibility of NDIC at International Associations

Since his assumption of office, Umaru Ibrahim had devoted time and energy to raise NDIC to greater heights even beyond the shores of Nigeria by strengthening collaboration and cooperation with the International Association of Deposit Insurers (IADI) and other sister deposit insurance agencies around the world. The NDIC is a founding member of IADI where under the leadership of Umaru Ibrahim, it enjoyed visibility at all events organised by the association. Umaru was elected into the Executive Council and served on its Audit Committee. This has brought a lot of opportunities to the NDIC particularly in the area of capacity building for its staff through seminars, workshops, and conferences. Based on the MD's outstanding performance at different IADI fora, the NDIC won the IADI award of the Best Deposit Insurance of the Year out of the 77 member institutions across the globe. It is the first deposit insurance agency to win the award in Africa since IADI commenced giving out such awards. In September 2018 when the NDIC hosted the Africa Regional Committee (ARC) Workshop in Lagos, Umaru Ibrahim was unanimously elected as the Chairman of the IADI-ARC.

In further recognition of his vast knowledge of deposit insurance and contributions to its development across the globe, Umaru Ibrahim was nominated to the Strategic Planning Working Group of the IADI in 2020 with a mission of developing a strategic plan that will guide the Association from 2022-2026.

In 2020, when the Corona Virus pandemic shut down the world, many organisations postponed planned events but the NDIC, the virile organisation it is, quickly adjusted to the new normal. As a matter of fact, during the pandemic, the corporation organised an international virtual conference attended by global stakeholders like the World Bank and IMF. It was the first of its kind on the African continent and showcased the corporation's readiness to face all challenges.

His passion to see NDIC emerge as a global leader in deposit insurance has seen NDIC formalise relationships with the deposit insurance agencies in Poland, Korea and Taiwan. Furthermore, he has welcomed several African nations to Nigeria to learn the processes of establishing and running a deposit insurance system. As a generous and selfless leader, he knows that the only way to achieve global financial stability is by equipping nations with the tools to succeed. It is with this positive attitude that he accepted the responsibility of establishing the African Centre for Deposit Insurance Studies in Abuja. He envisions the centre to be a world class institution for banking and deposit insurance learning.

Apart from IADI, the NDIC also established relationship with the Islamic Financial Services Board (IFSB) with headquarters in Malaysia. The IFSB is a standard setting body, which promotes the soundness and stability of the Islamic financial services institutions, which Nigeria now embraces.

Out of the MD's desire for excellent service delivery, he ensured that the NDIC got three International Standard Organisation (ISO) Certificates in Information Security Management, Business Continuity Management and IT Services. The ISO Certification is an international standard that helps organisations demonstrate excellence and best practice in achieving its mandate.

Legacy

Umaru spoke about the legacy he would like to leave behind after having served meritoriously at the NDIC. According to him, he would like to bow out and leave behind a solid, professional, highly-regarded, well-positioned organisation that would continue to earn its place, role and respect in the banking industry; a corporation that excels in its responsibility of protecting depositors, ensuring effective supervision of the banking system and also participating in the resolution of banking problems.

CHAPTER FOUR

IN THE EYES OF OTHERS

The comments of a few of Umaru's close associates represent the aggregate of opinion about what the majority thought of him. Those who knew him from his teenage day, those who came across him when he was a growing adolescent, those who he met at the workplace, and indeed all strata of human endeavours – everyone had kind words to say about him.

Yahaya Hamma is a former Secretary to the State Government of Kano State. He was also a Special Adviser to the late Head of State, General Sani Abacha. Hamma was also a three-time Director-General of the Muhammadu Buhari campaign organisation in 2003, 2007 and 2011.

Hamma has known Umaru as far back as his high school days when both of them were students and also when both of them started working. As a student, he described Umaru as a "very progressive young man". In his words, "I knew Umar Ibrahim's father as a judge in Wudil when Umaru himself was a young boy. Later, I came to know him as a growing young man in secondary school after I finished my secondary school and came to Rumfa College as an HSC student. We got very close because we were both members of the Muslim Student Association where I was President. Both of us were also members of the debating society where I was President as well. He was deeply interested in politics alongside the late Mohammed Sanusi Abubakar who was a lecturer and a newspaper columnist.

When Umaru started working, after school, he worked under Hamma who described him as a very diligent, very dedicated, very forthright worker. He said he enjoyed working with Umaru tremendously and those attributes made him draw Umaru even closer to himself to help him develop his leadership potential. In his words, "I saw in him the potential to become a leader either in the public or private sector, but more importantly in the public sector and I have not been disappointed on how he has turned out. After I left the public service of Kano State, he was already a Permanent Secretary until he himself resigned from State Service and joined the Federal Service."

Hamma thought that Umaru's progression in his career had been steady, stable and consistent because of his mental and managerial capacity. He said that it was not for nothing that he had risen to become the Chief Executive of the NDIC because Umaru had balanced his life and career development well. According to him, "I didn't see it as a windfall for him; I saw it as well-deserved for someone with his level of competence and integrity."

Hamma always had high expectations of Umaru. He believed that he would go far in his career and he said he had not been disappointed at how Umaru had fared. He ended by paying glowing tributes to Umaru as someone who has impressed him a lot.

Baba Gana Zanna is a former Director General of the National Directorate of Employment. He had the opportunity of meeting Umaru when both of them were course mates at the National Institute of Policy and Strategic Studies, Kuru, Jos in 2000.

He said that the first thing he observed about Umaru when they met was his calm and friendly disposition. They would later grow even closer to become good friends while at Kuru when they usually rode in the same car to and from Abuja during weekends. That gave Zanna further opportunity to know Umaru not only from an official perspective, but also on a personal level.

As course mates at Kuru, Zanna described Umaru as one of the leading scholars in class. He said that Umaru usually left no one in doubt about how brilliant he was when he would always come before the class to discuss given issues exhaustively.

According to him, he was not surprised that Umaru had risen to the apex of his career as the Managing Director of the NDIC. In his words, "Everything pointed to fact that barring any untoward vicissitude of life, his star will continue to shine."

Eminent economist, Dr. Shamsudeen Usman was a former Minister of Finance and National Planning. At various times, he was also a Deputy Governor of the Central Bank of Nigeria and the MD/CEO of NAL Merchant Bank.

Umaru and Usman attended the same primary school where Usman was his senior. He was also a year ahead of Umaru at the Ahmadu Bello University, Zaria. They would later go on to work together in their capacities as top officials of two key government regulatory institutions in the country. That was when both of them grew closer.

According to Usman, they worked together smoothly and seamlessly not only because they had known each other since their younger days, but also because by Umaru's natural disposition, he could work with anybody. He said that Umaru had an unobtrusive mien about him that made it easy for people to interact with him at various levels.

Looking back at their relationship, Usman had this to say: "Umaru is somebody who is very considerate and that is probably one of his important attributes. He treats everybody with respect irrespective of their cadre and he is not a guy who goes out looking for trouble; in fact, he abhors conflicts. Right from our younger days in school to date, I cannot remember anyone who has violently disagreed with him and vice versa. I cannot remember any such incident or person."

He ended by describing Umaru as one whose versatility was evident, judging by the way he had been able to successfully pilot the affairs of the NDIC to its present height even though he studied Political Science and not Economics.

"He is as good as the best," said Shamsudeen Usman. Dr. Garba Donli, who had known Umaru since 1992, spoke glowingly of him. They met at the NDIC training Centre that year when Umaru, as the Director of Personnel, declared open a workshop. However, Umaru incidentally had known him when he was an Examination Officer at ABU. Soon after the workshop, he got an invitation to see the erstwhile MD of the NDIC at the time and he was offered an appointment as a Deputy Director and Head of Training.

According to him, till this day, Umaru did not tell him that he got the NDIC job through his intervention but he had no doubt on his mind about how he got it.

Dr. Donli described Umaru as a completely detribalised Nigerian who released his children to boarding school far away at Adesoye College in Offa without fearing the possibility of wrong indoctrination.

Donli compared Umaru to an Army General who was always strategic in his thinking. He said Umaru always remained focused and kept his eyes on the ball in the pursuit of his objectives. According to him, "He has a way of clearing obstacles along the way, not by throwing tantrums but by his silent overwhelming tenacity."

Donli showered praises on Umaru for becoming the first career officer who, through a dint of hard work and efficiency, had risen to become the MD/CEO of the NDIC – a feat that was unprecedented in the history of the NDIC.

INDEX

A

Abang, Bernard, 70
Abba Abdullahi, 13
Abdullahi Mahmoud, 59
Abdulrahman Sambo, 51
Aboi Shekari, 38
Abuja, 84–85, 89, 100, 105
Adesoye College, 36–37, 107
Africa, 71–72, 95, 99
Africa Regional Committee (ARC), 100
AG (Action Group), 15
Ahmadu Bello University, 18, 27, 54, 105
Alkali Ibrahim Ahmed, 1, 8
Angola, 70, 75
armed forces, 69, 71

B

Bakolori Dam, 46
Balarabe Isma'ila, 51
Bala Usman, 20
Bank, Savannah, 81, 88
bank failures, 63, 89
banking, 53, 56, 100
banking industry, 65–66, 73, 87, 89, 97, 101
banking sector, 52–53, 64–65, 87, 94, 97
banking services, 65, 79, 90
banking system, 61, 65–68, 79, 86, 90, 98, 101
banks, 53, 60–62, 65–69, 78–82, 87, 90, 93, 95–99
  affected, 67, 79, 90
  country's, 98
  distressed, 68, 73
  failed, 79–81, 93–94

  healthy, 79–80
  state-owned, 81
Banks and Financial Institutions (BOFI), 79
Bauchi, 5, 89
Benin, 23–24
Board, 62, 76–77, 86–88, 96–98
Board of Directors, 77, 85–86
British colonialists, 15, 25

C

cabinet office, 29–30, 33, 38, 50–52, 54
Cairo, 37
Calabar, 25
CBN (Central Bank of Nigeria), 37, 53, 55, 59–60, 62, 66–68, 76, 79–80, 82, 86, 90, 95–97, 105
city, 4, 9–12, 16, 24–25
  growing, 10, 25
  largest, 10, 25
civilian administration, 38–40
civilian rule, 38, 77, 97
civilians, 34, 38
civil servants, 30–31, 34, 50, 55
civil service, 29–30, 47, 50, 53
civil war, 16, 18, 24–25
classes, 4, 12, 14, 16, 73, 105
conflicts, 74
  abhors, 106
corporation, 59, 64, 68, 77, 82–83, 85–97, 100–101
  young, 64, 68, 83
cost, 17, 79, 91
council, 30, 41
counter coups, 16
coup, bloody, 16
court, 7, 30, 81, 96
Craft School, 9, 13

D

Degema, 26-27
  new, 62-64, 77
  political, 38, 40
deposit insurance agencies, 53, 99-100
deposit insurance coverage, 78, 87
deposit insurance system, 53, 78, 100
Deposit Insurance System (DIS), 53, 78, 100
depositors, 53, 66, 69, 78-79, 88, 90, 95
deregulation, 65, 97
design, 37, 61
discharge, 61, 88
distress, 65, 68, 73
drought, 33, 71

E

Ebhodaghe, John, 59, 76, 97
Economics, 37, 106
economy, 53, 65, 80, 97-99
EDMS (Electronic Documents Management System), 92
education, 4, 9, 13, 18
  western, 8
emir, 1, 3-4, 10, 16, 43
Employment, 28, 35, 105
endeavours, human, 80, 103
Engineer Rabi'u Musa Kwankwaso, 46
engineers, 9, 45
Enugu, 23-25
environment, 7, 41, 74
era, apartheid, 72
essay, long, 71, 73
establishment, 5, 82
Europe, 72, 91
evenings, 26, 53
examination, 5, 61, 63

excellence, 74, 101
expertise, 32, 70-71
export, 25, 27
exposure, 3, 56, 62, 89
extra-curricular activities, 15-16
eye opener, 24, 33

F

facilitators, 73, 91
facilities, 19-20, 26, 85
factions, 41, 48
failure resolution, 77-78, 80-81
failures, 53, 78-79
FATB (First African Trust Bank), 68, 73
federal capital territory, 29, 55
Federal Deposit Insurance Corporation (FDIC), 62, 83
Federal Government, 31, 33, 43, 64, 71, 84
Federal Housing Authority (FHA), 84-85
Finance, 52, 56, 60, 85-86, 96, 105
  ministry of, 49, 51
financial services, 87, 90
financial services industry, 32, 65
financial system, 65, 78, 87, 93, 98
findings, 32, 39, 66, 72, 89
fiqh, 2-3
Foreign Affairs, 71-72
formats, 61-62
foundation, 10, 63, 93
framework, 61-62, 82, 93
Fridays, 16
Fulani, 2
functionaries, 52, 72
functions, 44, 53, 63, 98
funds, 33, 47, 66, 68, 98

G

Gaya, 1-2, 6-7, 41
General Abdulsalami Abubakar, 97
General Ibrahim Babangida, 53, 64
generality, 41, 65
General Murtala Mohammed, 14, 29, 38, 75
General Olusegun Obasanjo, 38, 75
General Yakubu Gowon, 22, 51
globe, 99-100
God, 35, 85
governance, 40, 50
  corporate, 82, 98
  good, 86
government, 2, 22, 24, 29-30, 40, 42, 44, 47-48, 50-52, 54
  colonial, 4-5
  military, 38, 49, 97
government house, 48-50
Governor, 40, 42, 44, 46, 49-50, 52, 56-57, 71, 80, 82, 96
  new, 29, 33, 49
Governor Abubakar Rimi, 40, 41-43, 48
Governor's Office, 52
graduates, 17, 22-23, 28
  fresh, 23, 50
graduation, 22, 24, 35, 50, 70, 76
ground, 21, 60
groundnuts, 6, 15
groups, 71-73
  small, 20, 60
growth, 18, 98
guidance, 36, 50, 56, 71, 86
guide, 62, 72, 83, 88, 100

H

head office, 84, 92
health, 36, 53, 61, 90
heart, 59, 73
heights, 94, 99, 106

helm, 32, 77, 86-87
history, 3, 22, 27, 107
homestead, 2, 9
hospitals, 31, 41, 63, 72
host, 14, 74
household, 3, 6, 8, 13
  large, 3, 8
Human Resource, 55, 77, 86

I

IADI (International Association of Deposit Insurers), 99-101
Ibadan, 10, 24, 27
Ibrahim, Umar, 103
ICSA (Interim Common Services Agency), 18
ICU. See intensive care unit
Ife, 24, 27
IFSB (Islamic Financial Services Board), 101
Imams, 2
IMF (International Monetary Fund), 62-63, 83, 100
institutions, 9, 18, 26, 60, 93, 95-96
  insured, 66, 82, 93
  new, 53, 65
  young, 28, 60
instrumental, 21, 57
integration, 19, 86
intensive care unit (ICU), 63
interface, 61, 86
International Associations, 83, 99
International Monetary Fund. See IMF
investors, 65, 73
  new, 67, 80
Isa Mohammed Argungu, 21-22
Islamic studies, 2-3
ISO (International Standard Organisation), 101

J

Jihad, 2
Jos, 25, 74, 76, 105
judiciary, 2, 10, 72
justice, 3, 31, 42
justification, 32, 42

K

Kaduna, 14, 19, 22, 25
Kano, 1-7, 9-14, 17, 19, 27, 30-31, 34, 37, 42-43, 49, 53-55, 64, 83
Kano city, 1, 3-4, 7, 9-11, 43, 47-48
Kano Civil Service, 52, 57
Kano emirate, 2, 6
Kano law school, 4
Kano Middle School, 14
Kano province, 1, 14
Kano State, 29, 41-42, 45-46, 55, 69, 103-4
Kano State Government, 20, 32-33, 45, 54-55
Kano State Students Association, 21
Kano State University, 9
Kuru, 69-70, 74, 105

L

Lagos, 24-25, 27, 29, 35, 37, 53, 55-56, 59, 64, 84, 89, 91, 100
law school, 4-5
leader, 15-16, 29, 38, 104
  national, 42, 48
leadership, 2, 11, 15-16, 28, 31, 33, 46, 74-75, 86, 94-95, 97, 99, 104
  right, 87, 97
learnt, 40, 62, 75, 98
lecturers, 20, 104
  guest, 70, 73-74
lectures, 17, 27, 70-71
lessons, 71, 98
letters, 33, 56-57
liberalisation, 65, 97
licenses, 82, 95
liquidate, 68, 97
liquidation, 68, 80-82, 84, 89, 97
liquidity problems, 62, 66
liquidity support, 67, 93
loans, 67, 82, 98-99
  non-performing, 82, 99
locations, 25, 90
loss, 8, 43, 46, 68
lucky, 50, 73-74, 95

M

Maiduguri, 6, 25, 36
Mallam Aminu Kano, 39, 42, 44, 48
management, 21, 61, 66, 73, 77, 82-83, 85, 87-89, 92-93, 96, 98
management team, 77, 86, 93
Managing Director, 8, 60, 76-77, 86-87, 105
  pioneer, 45, 59, 62, 76
Manchester University, 36-37
manpower development, 46, 83, 91
Master's Degree, 35-37
mates, 5, 21, 105
measures, radical, 41-42
Mecca, 4-5
Medicine, 36-37
military, 16, 70, 72-73, 75
military coup, 29, 31, 49
Military Governor, 29-31, 38
military regime, 38, 69, 81
millennium years, 76-77
mix, good, 12, 14
money, 15, 33, 65
monitor, 67, 78
moral obligation, 94
mosque, central, 11, 16
mother, 1, 3, 8
movement, 7, 9, 11, 64, 82, 85
MSSN (Muslim Students Society of Nigeria), 17, 19
mufti, 1, 6

N

Namibia, 72, 75
NANS (National Association of Nigerian Students), 23
National Assembly, 46, 49, 86
National Council of Nigerian Citizens (NCNC), 15
National Directorate, 35, 70, 105
National Institute, 69-70, 73-74, 76
National Institute of Policy and Strategic Studies. See NIPSS
National Party of Nigeria (NPN), 39, 44, 47
native authority, 7, 10, 12
natural disposition, 35, 106
NDE (National Directorate of Employment), 35, 70, 105
NDIC (Nigeria Deposit Insurance Corporation), 1, 53, 55-57, 59-69, 71, 73, 75-87, 89-97, 99-101, 104-7
NEPU (Northern Elements People Union), 11, 15
Nigeria, 10-11, 29-30, 53, 55, 59-60, 64, 68, 71-73, 75, 77, 80, 87, 94, 97, 99-101
Nigeria Deposit Insurance Corporation. See NDIC
Nigerian Army, 34, 43, 70
Nigerian banks, 53, 61
Nigerian economy, 53, 64
Nigerian Labour Congress, 47
Nigerian Peoples Party (NPP), 48
Nigerians, 5, 23, 25, 27, 41, 72
Nigerian universities, 17, 94
NIPSS (National Institute of Policy and Strategic Studies), 69, 71-75, 105
NNDC (Northern Nigerian Development Corporation), 32
Northern Nigeria, 9-10
Northern Nigerian Development Corporation. See NNDC

Northern Nigerian Government, 6, 9
Northern People Congress (NPC), 11, 15
Nsukka, 23-24, 27
NYSC (National Youth Service Corps), 22, 27-28

O

Offa, 36-37, 107
oil, 25, 64, 98
operations, 61, 79, 86, 88
operators, 90, 95
opposition, 15
organisations, 45-46, 61, 76, 95, 100-101, 103
overthrown, 31, 51
owners, 68, 82

P

panels, 33, 55
probe, 30-31
panic, 66-67
parents, 12, 20, 34
participants, 69-71, 73, 75
partner, 68, 83
party, 15, 21, 39, 41-42, 44, 47-49
regional, 15
passion, 74, 100
Permanent Secretary, 39, 48-52, 54, 56, 104
personnel, 32, 106
petitions, 30, 93, 96
police, 69-70, 73, 96
policies, 40, 61-62, 69, 72
political leadership, 29-30
political parties, 38-39, 41
politicians, 34, 71
politics, 16, 46, 104
polytechnics, 45-46
populace, 41, 65, 67
population, 3, 10, 12, 24, 28

port, 25, 33
Port Harcourt, 24–26, 28, 89
position, 35, 52, 56, 81, 96
   comfortable, 84
   strategic, 45, 98
President, 22, 74, 82, 84, 96, 104
projects, 31, 84, 89, 92–93
promotions, 38, 78
property, 85, 92
proposal, 5, 22
protection, 78–79, 89
Provincial Government Secondary School, 13–14, 17
provisions, 20, 31, 41, 64, 79
PRP (People Redemption Party), 39, 41–42, 44, 47–49
public confidence, 87, 90

Q

Qur'an, 3
Qur'anic School, 2–3

R

recapitalise, 82, 98
recognition, 93, 100
recommendations, 5, 39
regime, 31–32
   ousted, 31, 39
   previous, 29, 33, 50
region, northern, 5, 7
regulations, 30, 61, 78
reign, 4, 15, 64
representatives, 22, 73, 81, 88
reputation, 3, 55
request, 18, 82
residence, 19, 84
resources, 32, 40, 77
responsibilities, 32, 45, 51–52, 61, 87, 95, 100–101
retirement, 9, 30, 85
review, 89, 91–92
   upward, 78, 87

revocation, 81–82
Rimi Administration, 39, 41–44
Rivers State, 22, 24, 26–27
Rumfa College, 60, 104

S

Sani Abacha, 14, 97
Sani Bello, 29, 38–39
SAP (Structural Adjustment Programme), 53, 64–65
Sarkin Kano Muhammadu Sanusi, 10
SBS (School of Basic Studies), 18–21
   deposit insurance, 59, 79, 88
scholars, 3, 71, 73, 105
scholarship, 20–21
school, 2–5, 7–9, 12–17, 26–27, 31, 36–37, 41, 55, 72, 104, 106
   primary, 9, 11–13, 26, 105
seat, 29, 46
secondary schools, 11, 13–15, 27, 34, 51, 94, 104
secondment, 44, 51
Secretary, 38, 40, 42, 44–45, 51–52, 54, 71
   former, 83, 103
Secretary to the Military Government (SMG), 49, 55
sector, 65, 70, 98
   financial, 53, 65, 89
Senate, 81, 88
servants, public, 49, 51
services, 43, 91, 99, 101
Shamsudeen Usman, 105–6
Sharia, 5
Sharia Legal System, 5
Shehu Mohammed, 8, 53, 55, 57
Sheikh Usman Dan Fodio, 2
Sir Ahmadu Bello, 15
sisters, 8, 12, 93
software, 88, 90
Sokoto, 89
Sokoto State, 46

SRA (Students Representative Assembly), 21–22
staff, 16, 26, 45, 53, 59, 61–63, 69, 71, 76–77, 83–85, 91, 99
    pioneer, 60, 62
staff members, 62, 90
staff welfare, 83
State Civil Services, 69–70
State Executive Council, 33, 39
State House, 39, 42
State Service, 60, 104
students, 3, 5, 13–24, 26–28, 34, 103
Students Union, 22–23
student unionism, 21–22
Sule Yahaya Hamma, 38, 40, 44, 51

T

Tahir, Ibrahim, 20
Tarka, Joseph, 15
team, 33, 37, 73–74, 92
template, 62, 89
tenacity, 107
tension, 30, 33, 35, 67
tenure, 47, 76
top, 34, 49–50, 95
top officials, 30, 49, 51, 106
top position, 50, 54
tours, 27, 71–72
training, 4, 9, 61, 77, 88, 91, 106
transactions, 31, 79
tribes, 12, 14
TTC (Teacher Training College), 9

U

Umaru Ibrahim, 1, 49, 52–53, 87–89, 91–95, 99–100
Under-Secretary, 49–50
United Kingdom, 36–37, 46, 56
United Middle Belt Congress (UMBC), 15

university education, 18–19
Uthman, Muhammad, 60

V

vacuums, 85, 99
vested interests, 43–44
victims, 33, 49
villages, 2, 31, 94
Viscount Lewis Harcourt, 25

W

war, 18, 24
water, 40, 45, 85, 94
Water Resources and Engineering Construction Agency. See WRECA
Wheeler Commission, 31–32
White Paper, 32–33, 43
Wole Adewunmi, 59, 64
World Bank, 62–63, 83, 100
world tours, 71–72
World War, 10
WRECA (Water Resources and Engineering Construction Agency), 44–49, 51, 83
Wudil, 1, 7–8, 12, 103

Y

Yahaya Hamma, 51, 103
yan santsi, 42, 47–48
Yola, 89
youths, 23, 94

Z

Zaria, 18–19, 22–24, 27, 51, 54, 105
Zimbabwe, 75
zonal offices, 89, 92

www.ingramcontent.com/pod-product-compliance
Lightning Source LLC
Chambersburg PA
CBHW051616230426
43668CB00013B/2123